# HOPE WHEN IT HURTS: THE SCARS THAT SHAPE US

## A CHRISTIAN WRITERS' COLLECTION (LARGE PRINT EDITION)

MICHAEL LACEY ELENAH KANGARA PAM PEGRAM
MIMI EMMANUEL JODI ARNDT ANGIE WALTHALL
MEREDITH SWIFT MIRANDA J. CHIVERS
J. MATTHEW KING KATHRYN SPRINGMAN JILL ROGERS
A. AINSWORTH EMILY SMITH KELLY WALK HINES

Edited by
MICHAEL LACEY

Story Builds

CREATIVE

# CONTENTS

# SNIPPETS

## IS THIS REALLY HAPPENING? (PAM PEGRAM)

During our hard seasons, we can become lost in our pain. But God has promised to use all things for good in our lives if we trust Him—even our struggles. He will use them to grow us and draw us closer to Him.

Our painful times can become precious as we learn what it means to abide, to develop intimacy with our Lord and to learn to live for Him. No matter the circumstance, He is enough to carry us through.

## LIFT YOUR EYES (ELENAH KANGARA)

Hope is the light from the lighthouse that ignites audacious faith. Little by little, the sun overtakes the darkness until it reaches full light. It just happens. When you hope, you do the same. The light for a dangerous faith emerges. You believe the impossible. The light from the lighthouse changes the faith of a sinking sailor. With hope, he is saved. Hope stirs you to desire. When desire is activated, the heavens open and pour out. Hope is the energy that lifts you up when everything inside of you wants to give up. Hope is the best friend, pointing you to the light at the end of the tunnel. So, hope you must.

## MY HOPE IS YOU (JODI ARNDT)

I know that the God I serve is mighty, and He will not fail. Even if he does not save me from circumstances, I will hope in Him alone. Even when things don't go as I planned, I know Jesus is the only way. I can be scarred, bruised, and battered, but with Jesus as my hope, I will never be abandoned.

What in your own life is God calling you to look at with new eyes? Is there pain that can push you toward Him?

## HOPE FOR THE MOMENT (MICHAEL LACEY)

Have you ever lost a job, had to live on savings, had multiple cars break down at once, been sick with the entire family, struggled in your marriage, felt insecure daily (sometimes hourly), and it just seems you can't catch a break...just a snowball of unfortunate events?

No? Just me? Okay. I guess you can skip this one. But if you need hope for the moment (and more), read this devotional.

## IT'S AMAZING WHAT YOU CAN LIVE THROUGH (ANGIE WALTHALL)

We are all terminal; none of us will get out of this alive, unless Jesus comes back first. Don't live in fear. Live in a way that makes others wonder what you've got and want it. The scars you accumulate along the way just give you a platform to share the goodness of the LORD.

## TRUSTING GOD THROUGH TURMOIL AND TRAUMA (MEREDITH SWIFT)

My elder daughter Sarah is non-verbal autistic. She is a strong and energetic young woman who usually enjoys robust good health. But in 2016, Sarah was stricken with a very serious illness.

In a time of intense pain and suffering—for all of us, and especially for Sarah, I felt as though I was navigating my way through a minefield. Even though I continued to speak with and pray to Him, I felt very disconnected from Jesus. I was lying in bed one night angrily demanding that God tell me why this was all happening. No answer. Tears of anguish and frustration poured out of me. And finally, when I was spent, I remember saying, "I don't know why You are doing this, but I am going to trust You".

## YOU ARE GOOD ENOUGH (MIMI EMMANUEL)

Stop beating yourself up, yes, you, right now. Stop beating yourself up about not being a good enough boss, employer, wife, husband, partner, whatever. You are good enough. Stop judging yourself and others; ask our Heavenly Father to help you be the best you can be, and do your best; that is good enough.

## HOPE IN THE DARKNESS (KELLY WALK HINES)

When I was just three years old, my mother was killed by her boyfriend. This was just the beginning of a chaotic, heartbreaking time that I would call my childhood.

But I realized the legacy that blesses me the

most is that my children are carrying on my mission and making it theirs.

This just makes whatever battles I overcame to get here feel worth it. I challenge you to think of your legacy. What do you strive to bring to the table? I pray you always find Hope in the Darkness.

## REAL BIBLICAL HOPE (MATTHEW KING)

Hope in the Bible is an extremely powerful word and incredibly vital to our understanding of God and His plan for us. Unfortunately many do not fully understand how the Scriptures use hope and therefore we risk losing its meaning. We will examine the true way hope is used in the Bible so that it can help uplift and grow our faith.

## WALKING WITH GOD (KATHRYN SPRINGMAN)

Once upon a time, in 1917 to be exact, a girl named Sarah was born. Her parents were farmers who had come to Oklahoma as children in the land run of 1889. All who knew Sarah adored her. However, her uncle knew that she was more than Sarah. She was Susie. He told her mother that, and both her parents tried to dissuade him. But the name Susie stuck and she was known as Susie to all who loved her. And that was many.

## FROM TRAUMA TO HOPE (JILL ROGERS)

It all started one night when I was twenty-three years old in a relatively new marriage. I wasn't feeling well, so my husband went off to play volleyball alone.

I assumed the knock at the door was my husband, but I was wrong. I opened the door to a strange man standing in the darkness ready to thrust in. With a swift move, there was a knife at my throat...

Since then, I got help in many ways and it took some time. Little by little, my life has come along to the place where my husband and I are helping others get healed from hurts and trauma in their lives. We can never be hopeless about anything that happens to us when we pray and bring God on the scene.

## HOPE IN THE WAITING (MIRANDA J. CHIVERS)

In 2002, a health crisis changed my life forever. After two years of riding the medical merry-go-round with chronic unrelenting pain and fatigue, I was frustrated, angry, and exhausted. As the swelling increased around my neck, I struggled to breathe, and my voice croaked.

## DRIVEN TOWARD HOPE (AL AINSWORTH)

If hope was to rise from our circumstances, it had to come from beyond me. When I am helpless, when I have exhausted my last option, He still has resources I can't even imagine. Our hope as believers is found in the person of Jesus Christ.

## HOPE, PEACE, AND CANCER-FREE (EMILY SMITH)

I see God's handiwork in creating me to be who He has called me to be. Little did I know that as an adult my voice would be needed for such a time as this? Facing the unknown I would use my voice to take a stand against an Enemy who was after my life.

## WHEN HOPE SEEMS LOST (PAM PEGRAM)

There is much in this world that can tempt us to lose sight of our hope and instead enter into a place of despair.

But now, we can be so confident because the

love of God has been poured out. Hope has a name, and His name is Jesus.

## THE GARDEN OF HOPE (MICHAEL LACEY)

The garden of hope requires praise foremost, then as consequence of praise: grace, wisdom, faith, and proper perspectives. Praise is the prescription for hope.

# INTRODUCTION

Hope for the Moment has truths for both women and men, though the majority of writers are women. It is a devotional collection from various authors around the world. You may notice different spellings or styles such as "Savior" versus "Saviour". We celebrate the international feel and have retained author styles.

Additionally, the viewpoints of each author do not reflect those of everyone involved. We differ on some theological issues, but our goal is to come together—despite those differences—to share messages of HOPE.

TRIGGER WARNING: this collection has some heavy topics (though they all point to the hope of God) including miscarriages, cancers, death of loved ones, suicide, and more.

DISCLAIMER: *if you have any issues with the theologies (which do vary slightly), or any devos in particular, please reach out to those authors directly. Each of us are passionate about the Word of God, and if we are risking blasphemy or causing damage in any way, we WANT to know. God's word is holy, and it deserves our best. Each writer is allowed to share their beliefs in a judgment-free way.*

However, this core belief holds true for all of us: salvation (and thus eternity in heaven with God) is available to all who call upon the name of Jesus. The deep, personal stories in this collection will inspire and encourage anyone with an open heart.

May the real stories from these real people reflect the real God and add hope to your season. There is hope, a living hope in Jesus and one that does not disappoint. You are not alone. You are loved. You are here for a reason.

Godspeed,

-Michael Lacey, Story-Builds.com (and the Christian Writers' Collections group)

THIS COLLECTION HAS PROMPTED A RELEASE OF A DEVOTIONAL STUDY JOURNAL CALLED THE HOPE GARDEN, AVAILABLE NOW.

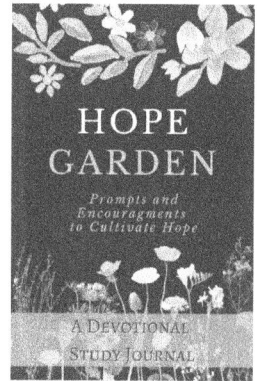

# THANKS TO YOU, THE READERS

Half of the proceeds from each Devo Writers Collaboration goes to a related charity for the first year of each book release. This HOPE devotional collection has supported Star of Hope, a Christ-centered community dedicated to meeting the needs of homeless men, women and their children.

So, we collectively shout, "THANK YOU!" for your 'donation', and we HOPE you draw nearer to God through these heartfelt writings.

~

To get first dibs on each new collection, as well as more freebies, join our mailing list at ChristWriters.com

# IS THIS REALLY HAPPENING? BY PAM PEGRAM

As the alarm sounded, I gasped as the realization hit me all over again. *Oh God, is this really happening? Is this real or is it all just a bad dream? How did I get here?* As I sat up, I immediately felt a tear trail down my face. My head throbbed and I had no desire to get up and go about my day. I sat, slumped in my bed, with what felt like the weight of the world on my shoulders.

It didn't really matter how I was feeling; I had responsibilities. I had to get it together. The kids needed to get up and get ready for school. They needed me. They had their own pain to deal with and they needed their mom to show up for them. Yet, I sat frozen. I was dazed and confused, still finding it hard to believe. My happily ever after had imploded once again. Divorce #2, *how could that be?* I had been happy for fourteen years and never saw this coming. We had this incredible family, this incredible life; everything was so good. What happened? How would I get through this? How could I go on with my life as a single mom of 3?

My devotional lay on my nightstand, stacked on top of my Bible. *Not today,* I thought. I was too exhausted to care what God had to say. I stared at it, mumbling under my breath, *I know! I need You, Lord, more than ever.* So, I reached for it, begrudgingly flipped it open and began to read about someone who was overwhelmed by the affliction in her life. "I can relate," I sarcastically whispered. I went on to read about how she stood before an overgrown garden full of weeds and grass. She was reminded that the gardener stops pruning the vines, pulling the weeds and mowing the grass when He no longer expects anything from the garden during that season. The scripture on the page was John 15:2:

> *Every branch in Me that does not bear fruit He takes away. Every branch that bears fruit, He prunes, that it may bear more fruit."*

The story illustrated how God uses our struggles and trials to prune or cleanse us, grow us or prepare us, so we will bear fruit for Him. The next sentence leapt off the page at me. "Shall I leave you alone?" *What? What did that say?* "Shall I leave you alone?" What a profound question. *No, that is not what I want,* I thought. The realization hit me. While we are not eager to invite hard times into our lives, we certainly dare not ask God to just leave us alone. If we never experience anything hard, how can we grow or become stronger or even learn to truly trust in and lean on God? How would we ever come to know how good He is?

The days, weeks, and months ahead were some of the most difficult in my life. I was heartbroken and, quite frankly, heartsick. Weight fell off my small frame and people wondered if I had a chronic illness. No – just devastated by my life circumstances. I would put on a brave face and get the kids out the door and off to school. Then, most mornings I would fall on my face on the floor and sob. One morning as I lay there sobbing out loud, crying out to God, I suddenly became aware that I was not alone. Jesus was laying right beside me. Now my eyes did not see Him, but my spirit did. I knew. I knew that I knew that I knew He was there laying right beside me.

It was in the most difficult time of my life that I realized that Jesus is enough. I had been in the process of accumulating what I thought I needed – a man, children, success, financial security, a fabulous home with a pool – and feeling pretty good about it when it all came tumbling down. You see, I loved Jesus. I had accepted Him as my Savior, but I lived for me, and my flesh wanted more. But here, during this devastating time, I learned that all I needed, truly needed, was Jesus. He is everything I have ever wanted, everything I will ever need. He is enough.

Jesus was enough to carry me through that hard season. I became aware of His presence and experienced Him in ways I had never known. Sometimes as people were speaking to me, I wanted to reply, "I hear you, Jesus." Prayers were answered in the craziest of ways. I came to understand that He is my strength, my fortress, and my rock. Even as I struggled to live out my faith, He remained faithful and fulfilled His promises to me. But... there was more to learn, more to understand.

*Abide in Me, and I in you. As the branch cannot bear fruit of itself, unless it abides in the vine, neither can you, unless you abide in Me."*
*-John 15:4*

As I studied the passages in John 15, I read about *abiding in Jesus* and I knew that is what He wanted from me. Abide means to dwell, to settle in, to sink deeper. I needed to sink deeper in my relationship with Jesus, to get to know Him in a more intimate way and to learn how to live for Him. To abide in Him, I would need to walk in obedience to Him. That meant studying God's word and understanding what He was asking me to do. Reading the Scripture of the day or relying on my pastor to tell me what God's word said would no longer be enough. I would need to invest in this relationship. Jesus had already proven He was all in; now I needed to be all in as well.

Abiding would mean learning to put Jesus first in my life. Oh, I would have told you what every good Christian girl says, "God first, family second, and then career." However, that was not true for me. I struggled and remember even questioning how I was supposed to love Him most. But as I got to know Jesus more, I soon discovered that it is only when we put Jesus first that we can become who we are meant to be, fulfill the purpose He has for us, become the wife our husband deserves, the mom our children need, and the friend so many crave. I came to believe the part in verse 5 that says, *"for without Me you can do nothing."*

> *If you abide in Me, and My words abide in you, you will ask what you desire, and it shall be done for you. By this My Father is glorified, that you bear much fruit; so you will be My disciples."*
> -John 15:7-8

Oh, the pruning process was painful. There was a cutting away of me and my selfish desires. Today, if I am not diligent in seeking Jesus, those still try to take root and spring forth. Satan wants us to believe that we need things over Jesus and that our security is in worldly assets, but nothing could be farther from the truth. As the Scripture above reminds us, as we obey His word and abide in His love for us, we come to experience and to understand His love more and more. The more time I spent in God's word, the more it got into me and radically transformed me and my life. My greatest desire today is to fulfill His desires for me and for my life to glorify my heavenly Father.

I can remember my oldest daughter sitting on

the steps in our home and telling me, "Mom, I don't know how, but God will use all of this for good." I smiled and nodded, but just couldn't see it then. Once I got on the other side of that devastating time and looked back, I could see Him and His ways so clearly. What an awesome God we serve. He has used my pain to draw me to Him; my story to bring glory to Him; and turned my test into my testimony. Because of this hard season, I know Jesus in a way I might not have ever known Him on this side of heaven. I love Him with all my being and long to inspire others to fall in love with Him, so that they might inspire others to fall in love with Him and on and on. As crazy as it sounds, I am thankful for the pain, because what it has brought me is precious.

~

Pam Pegram is an author, blogger, speaker and a Bible study leader. She loves to come together with others to study God's Word, gain understanding, and walk in obedience to it. She is passionate about helping others recognize that their value, worth and the love the Creator

has for them stays intact no matter what they have endured or what they have done. She wants everyone to know they can live loved! Her greatest desire is to inspire others to fall in love with Jesus so that they might inspire others. She leads workshops and retreats and speaks to groups large and small.

Pam is a Legacy Leader with DVTD®—a Marketplace with a Mission. After serving as a Senior Leader with Premier Designs jewelry for 22 years, they transitioned in a new company where every purchase gives back to ministries and humanitarian causes, making a difference to stop human trafficking, send Bibles to areas not open to the gospel, employee homeless teens, provide clean water and soap to those without it, support mental illness programs, fund missionaries and so much more.

Pam is married to Tom and they live in North Mississippi where they love spending time with their family and friends.

Her book *Saved by Grace, Now What?* focuses on discovering how to have an intimate relationship with your Savior.

Go to pampegram.com to subscribe to Pam's blog, *Master What Matters*. Also visit pampegram. com/unstuck to subscribe to her FREE video series to discover steps you can take to move out

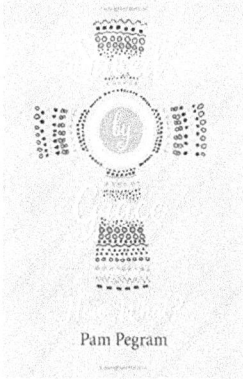

Pam Pegram

of your stuck places and into the plan God has for you. And don't forget to follow her @pampegram on Facebook and Instagram.

Get Pam's book today: https://amzn.to/3n2dgnD

# LIFT YOUR EYES BY ELENAH KANGARA

elson Mandela said a winner is a dreamer who refuses to give up. Because hope saved me so many times, I made up my mind to refuse to give up. Hope is Refusing To Give Up. I have experienced that if you refuse to give up hoping, no matter what has happened to you that is disappointing, God will give you double for your trouble!

Today, I am writing not for the world to see, but just for you to see. I am sent to you by God to prophesy to EVERY dry bone. In my right hand, I am holding a special antidote for you, called hope.

> *Every valley shall be raised up, every mountain and hill made low; the rough*

*ground shall become level, the rugged places*
*a plain. And the glory of the* LORD *will be*
*revealed, and all people will see it together.*
*For the mouth of the* LORD *has spoken."*
*-Isaiah 40:4-5 NIV*

God sees you.

Like a wounded soldier, a warrior, you daily look up at the sky to see where the sun is, trying to remember where the sun was before you fell. You try to get back to your feet, but it hurts so badly where you've been hit. It feels like your world has been hit (your relationships, marriage, finances, health, career, ministry, and purpose down to the last breath). The world has gotten darker and scarier; the captains of its winds cannot be trusted. Waking up hurts, it seems easier for you to slide and hide in unconsciousness. You smile, but you want to cry. You speak bravely, but your words do not reconcile with your reality. You look so confident, only because daylight demands it. When the sun sets, you cannot hide it anymore, you don't try to look away, you don't bury your face; you let the tears of uncertainty run down your face. You feel all alone as you look around trying to shut out the whispers of despair. Dear child of God, be encouraged; you are a warrior. You are born to win.

Lift up your eyes to the sky. Listen; you are not alone. Where does your help come from? Your Heavenly Father sees what is trying to invade the life within you; the fears, the discouragement, the secret tears, and even the corners of your doubts. Like a voice of hope in the wilderness of loss, God has lifted me up and has sent me running to you. I am sent on a mission to rescue a warrior, with tools for you to rise and shine!

**LISTEN. FOR YOU, IT IS DECREED TO ONLY GET BETTER!**

> *But the God of all grace, who hath called us unto his eternal glory by Christ Jesus, after that ye have suffered a while, make you perfect, stablish, strengthen, settle you."*
> *-1 Peter 5:10 KJV*

You are in the aftermath of having suffered, and it can only get better and best. That is your portion into His eternal glory allotted to you by grace.

I speak restoration into your life. I speak Restitution! I prophesy not only is God restoring your years, but that which you lost is here topped up with interest for you. Not only are you healed but wholeness is yours. Not only are you growing spiritually, but you will fulfill God's purpose in this land of the living! Not only is that debt gone, but you will lend to nations. Life in full is yours, take it! Listen, I am speaking as God gives it to me for you. Today, salvation comes to you, as hope.

## WHY IS HOPE SO IMPORTANT?

> *For in this hope we were saved. But hope that is seen is no hope at all. Who hopes for what they already have? But if we hope for what we do not yet have, we wait for it patiently."*
> *-Romans 8:24-25*

Hope is the light from the lighthouse that ignites audacious faith. Little by little, the sun overtakes the darkness until it reaches full light. It just happens. When you hope, you do the same. The light for a dangerous faith emerges. You believe the impossible. The light from the lighthouse changes the faith of a sinking sailor. With hope, he is saved. Hope stirs you to desire. When desire is activated, the heavens open and pour out. Hope is the energy that lifts you up when everything inside of you wants to give up. Hope is the best friend, pointing you to the light at the end of the tunnel. So, hope you must.

## EMBRACE THE GIFT OF HOPE.

So, I hear you asking, "What do I do, Mrs.

Elenah, when the future looks bleak? What do I do when all I've tried has failed? What do I do when nothing seems to work?" You lost it all and even your confidence is rejecting you. In the face of the impossible, what do you do?

I'll tell you what I did. When the doctors said, "There is no more heartbeat, you can't give birth to that child," I quickly engaged in a spiritual activity of expecting something good. I opposed the negative. That's how we hope! Because of hope, I became confident of this very thing, that He who had begun a good work in me was able to perfect it! (Philippians 1:6) Audacious faith took over.

I started receiving. I knew I already had "it" inside of me. With all that I had, I received what God had already given me, that child. Where did I get the energy to receive? Let me tell you. I got that as a GIFT of HOPE. I focused on the hope that with God, I can only win. So today, your first job is to receive the gift of HOPE. This is what you need to start desiring and receiving. Hope is direction for your life. Meditate on hope, confess it, declare it, decree it, and expect good.

True hope is a gift that comes from God. Psalm 62:5 says, "Yes, my soul, find rest in God; my hope comes from Him." Cultivate receiving the gift of hope like a child, with anticipation and excitement. May the gift of hope lead you to see your future in a bright way, defeating every darkness. May hope lead you to an excitement that surpasses all understanding. May hope activate the audacity of faith that moves the mountains you are facing right now.

**PRAY WITH ME, SAY,**

"Father, God, I appreciate you and thank you for the precious gift of Hope. I repent from living a life staring at your precious gift and not recognizing it.

Today, I pray that you open my spiritual eye so I can see this gift clearly. I am done living in the dark. I am done chasing the wind. I am done living life apart from You.

I promise, Dad, that by the help of the Precious Holy Spirit, I will treasure and protect every gift You have placed in me. I hold You dear, I hug hope dearly, my heart beats deeply and truly only for You.

Thank You for perfecting everything that concerns me. In the precious name of Jesus Christ, Amen."

**HOPE AND PERSPECTIVE PERCEPTION.**

When you hope, you invite fresh perspectives. Fresh perspectives bring about unprecedented innovation! Those who hope in the Lord will renew their strength. (Isaiah 40:31)

In the twinkling of an eye, your life begins to change the minute your perspective perception changes. The devil is an expert at playing all kinds of movies in your mind. If you allow the devil's falsity to keep on playing, it can take you down into the dark hole with your eyes wide open. But if you change your perspective perception, your hope and light come on just like a click.

In Chapter 8 of my book, *Supernal Grace,* I discuss in detail perspective perception. I write that nothing exists until we perceive it. We give perspective to that which we perceive to be real or substantial in our lives. What we experience in life can give birth to our memories. The ways in which those memories exist depend upon our perspective perception. We must perceive in a way that challenges a limited perspective that dries out hope. If we do this, we can confront challenges, ideas, doctrines, and even established wrong theology to access success from the root of our problems. Nothing kills hope and squanders our time and keeps us from embracing new and exciting opportunities like the wrong perspective perception! In my personal experiences, the moment I stopped giving the past and challenges around me an identity through perception, hope took over. Everything started to melt: the pain, the grief, the hurts, all gone!

God promises to give us hope. Situations can change. It's only the lie from the pits of hell that says if things are bad, they will not change, and if things are good, it's not going to last. The enemy of your success is bent on decreasing your hope until you are hopeless. He likes for you to lean towards the negative.

Here are a few things you can begin to do, right now, to maintain the right perspective perception:

**Attitude and Talk**

Defeat your circumstances by your attitude – choose joy always and be content. Choose the joy of the Lord, not the joy of circumstances. Go help somebody, laugh, jump up and down. Monitor your speech. Don't talk about what the devil is doing, talk about what Jesus is doing. (Philippians 4:11)

**Meditate**

One thing that has changed my whole life is meditation. Meditate on the word of God, on whatever is good, then meditate on the love of God some more. Nothing can separate us from His love. Meditate and receive God's love. (Philippians 4:8)

**Focus on what you already have**

Know your Gift and use your talents to support your gift. Don't get busy comparing yourself with somebody – Be you. You are fearfully and wonderfully made. (Psalm 139:14)

### Be a Prisoner of Hope

Choose to be a prisoner of hope – locked up with hope until it saturates your subconscious mind. Refuse to give in to whispers of lies that constantly tell you to give up! "Return to your fortress, you prisoners of hope, even now I announce that I will restore twice as much to you." (Zechariah 9:12)

### Finally, Be Patient With Yourself

I love fermenting foods. When you start the fermenting process, with a little patience, after a few days, you start to see little bubbles rising in your ferment. Then you know something is alive and teaming up with healthy bacteria, ready to take up residence in your body and help keep pathogens at bay!

Just like fermentation, there are circumstances in our lives that become better and better with time and patience. The process of fermentation may take a long time, but if you allow the process, fermentation not only makes food taste better but increases your gut health, the digestive system's health, and enhances the immune system. Just because some things seem to be taking a long time to happen in your life does not mean that nothing is happening. Meditate on enjoying every single process. Celebrate every progress, no matter how small.

In our home we take Communion, almost every day, to celebrate Jesus, life, and whatever milestones. Hear this word and believe it: God never sleeps or slumbers. Everything Is Working Together For Your Good! You may be going through what you are going through because sometimes God must do something IN you before He does something THROUGH YOU. So, expect good news. Don't be afraid to hope. Be a little patient with yourself, relax, and take a deep breath. Say out loud: "Everything is working together for my good!"

Like Job, wait patiently for your appointed time. Let every dry bone live!

> If a man die, shall he live (hope) again?
> all the days of my appointed time will I
> wait (hope), till my change come."
> -Job 14:14 KJV

~

Elenah Kangara is a business woman, an author, speaker, and teacher with a heart for discipling nations in the areas of meditation, healing, and prophetic gifts. The Texas resident is the award winning, bestselling author of *Supernal Grace*.

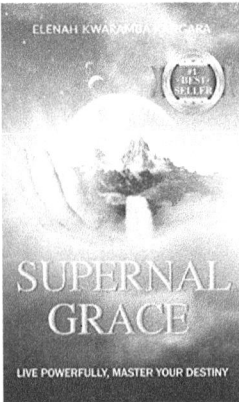

Get your copy of Supernal Grace today: https:/amzn.to/3l7SCRf

# MY HOPE IS YOU BY JODI ARNDT

S hadrach, Meshach, and Abednego replied, "O Nebuchadnezzar, we do not need to defend ourselves before you. If we are thrown into the blazing furnace, the God whom we serve is able to save us. He will rescue us from your power, Your Majesty. But even if he doesn't, we want to make it clear to you, Your Majesty, that we will never serve your gods or worship the gold statue you have set up."
-Daniel 3:16-18 NLT

Reading this passage when I was younger, I

focused on how God rescued Shadrach, Meschach, and Abednego from the fiery furnace. It took many years for me to turn my attention to the most important statement:

> But even if he doesn't, we want to make it clear to you, Your Majesty, that we will never serve your gods or worship the gold statue you have set up."

Even as a kid and young adult, I felt confident there were no leaders I would worship or other religions I would follow. The portion that sticks out to me now is that God is worthy of our worship even when bad things happen. God would still have been God if He didn't save these men.

A few years ago, my mom was diagnosed with breast cancer. By God's tremendous grace they caught it early, removed it, and she is in remission. Now I can breathe easier, knowing she is not in immediate or impending danger. But at the time, the torture of uncertainty and potential loss of my mama was suffocating. To open my eyes every day and remember that I could lose her, to have that weight slam into my chest each morning as I woke, seemed unbearable.

If I did not have Jesus, it would have consumed

me. Without Jesus, this world is bleak and dark. Without Jesus, there is no hope. He is our Hope. Jesus is the sweet drop of honey in a bitter situation. Somehow He held my heart and whispered in my ear: "I love you, and I am holding you, no matter what."

I remember driving to the hospital for her surgery, tears streaming down my face, as two songs came on the radio. These two songs were my anthems that carried me through months of pain and uncertainty.

The first was "I Have This Hope" by Tenth Avenue North, and the second was "Even If" by MercyMe:

"I have this hope
In the depth of my soul
In the flood or the fire
You're with me and You won't let go"
-Tenth Avenue North


"I know You're able and I know You can
Save through the fire with Your mighty hand
But even if You don't
My hope is You alone
I know the sorrow, and I know the hurt
Would all go away if You'd just say the word
But even if You don't

My hope is You alone"
-Mercy Me

The Lord showed Himself to me that day in the car, speaking to my heart that He is good no matter what, and I can put my hope in Him. Even when everything around me crumbles and fades, I can know that my God does not. Although my feelings tell me the hurt will never go away, I can trust that my God will never leave me. Even if my mom had not made it, I know that God is still worthy of my praise and my life should be lived in worship to Him.

Pain always pushes us in some way. It may push us to action when we otherwise may have remained still. It can pull us away from things that are hurting us, helping us realize the need to protect ourselves. Pain can quiet us, make us focus on what is important, revealing what is truly necessary. Pain can be a reminder that no one and nothing else but Jesus can satisfy fully. If we focus only on the pain, it can isolate us. If we dwell on ourselves and how much it hurts, our gaze downward and inward, we can be devoured by it. Oh, but if we lean into Jesus, how pain can clear our vision.

I had to make a choice. I knew that if I focused on the bad that could happen, I would drown in it.

The Holy Spirit gently nudged me, showing me I couldn't dwell on it. I could sit in sadness and wallow, but I refused. He had more. More for her, more for me, more for the rest of this life.

I tend to take things for granted, as we all do, when things are going well. It's easy to get caught up in the day to day, forgetting your blessings. Sometimes it's only by the threat of losing those blessings that we truly come to appreciate them. I praise God that He is allowing me to have more time with my mom, for my kids to have their grandma. Knowing what she went through and how we could have lost her shifted my mind and my heart. It's not that I didn't treasure her before, but moreso that I needed to see more clearly. The tiny bit of faith I had, Jesus took it and increased it. If it had not been for that experience, my trust in the Lord today would not look the same.

I know I will have pain again. I know I will lose. I know that the darkness will press in again, trying to tell me to give up. But I know that the God I serve is mighty, and He will not fail. Even if he does not save me from circumstances, I will hope in Him alone. Even when things don't go as I planned, I know Jesus is the only way. I can be scarred, bruised, and battered, but with Jesus as my hope, I will never be abandoned.

What in your own life is God calling you to

look at with new eyes? Is there pain that can push you toward Him?

God, You are mightier than the thunder of the great waters, mightier than the breakers of the sea —the Lord on high is mighty! (Psalm 93:4) Lord, I thank you for the blessing of pain. If it weren't for pain, I may not realize my desperate need for You. You are Holy and Glorious, and worthy of all my praise, regardless of circumstances. I thank You for Your grace. May we remember Your goodness, O Lord, and cling to You in every situation.

～

Jodi Arndt was raised out in the country in the bootheel of Missouri, where farmland is prevalent and so is hospitality. She is the youngest of three, with two older brothers. Jodi played sports throughout her education and her first job was on a potato farm. She played outside, loved the open sky, and dreamed of creating something special someday.

Jodi grew up in the church but as she matured, she found herself searching for more. In high school she found a youth group where she discovered her desire to deepen her relationship with Jesus.

Jodi completed her education at Southwest Baptist University in Bolivar, Missouri obtaining her degree in Business Administration with a concentration in Marketing/Management. This is where she met Stefan and her heart was captivated. She dated him for five years and have now been married over ten years.

Jodi is now a mama to three spirited boys who grow her faith and her heart daily. With rough-housing sessions in the living room floor and legos underfoot, Jodi finds refuge from the masculinity with her (girl) dog, Izzy. In a house full of boys you'd think Jodi would feel out of place, but she is happy and at home in the cuddly arms of her husband and sons. Jodi homeschools her boys and and watches the St. Louis Cardinals in her remaining spare moments. She is active with her church family, teaching Sunday School and Vacation Bible School.

If you are interested in finding out more about Jodi, you can get to know her better through her blog "Mommy-hood Musings" at jodiarndt.com.

Get Jodi's book, Little Moments, Big God, today: https://amzn.to/3ilB9mk

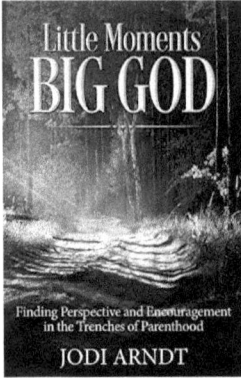

# HOPE FOR THE MOMENT BY MICHAEL LACEY

Why would you want to hear from me about hope? Maybe you shouldn't. Maybe you should just skip this and find something that doesn't challenge you, something that is easier to read, shorter, more exciting.

Have you ever lost a job, had to live on savings, had multiple cars break down at once, been sick with the entire family (costing nearly a month's time and money), struggled in your marriage, felt insecure daily (sometimes hourly), and it just seems you can't catch a break...just a snowball of unfortunate events?

No? Just me? Okay. I guess you can skip this one after all.

When I was asked to write about hope, I was

initially excited, but it faded just as quickly as I thought about where my family is in life. I'm about to get real honest, so hold on tight. But I'm also going to give you the secret to hope. And in keeping with the subtitle of this devotional collection, I'll share with you the physical scar that has helped shape my own hope.

I grew up in church, mostly, and learned to love God and His word. Did I mention I'm currently a worship leader? Going on 12 years now. Even while working for the church, doing the Lord's work, my family is struggling! Can you believe that? Well, it's all right here, in Romans 5 (a section surely used through many devotionals in this collection... at least I *HOPE* so... sorry, I'm a dad now, so I can make those kinds of jokes).

> Therefore, since we have been declared righteous by faith, **we have peace with God** through our Lord Jesus Christ. 2 We have also obtained access through Him by faith into this grace in which we stand, and we rejoice in the hope of the glory of God. 3 And not only that, but we also **rejoice in our afflictions**, because we know that **affliction produces endurance**, 4 **endurance produces**

**proven character**, and **proven character produces hope**. 5 *This hope will not disappoint us*, because God's love has been poured out in our hearts through the Holy Spirit who was given to us."

-Romans 5:1-5, CSB (emphasis added)

How beautiful is that?! Challenging? Yes, but so encouraging.

"What's the problem?" you ask.

Well... glance back up at verse 3. It starts with "afflictions," or as other versions say, "tribulations." I am deep in the middle of tribulations. How so? Let's take a quick snapshot, and mind you, I'm leaving a lot out:

- I lost/left one of my main jobs about a year ago, *hoping* that God had something waiting for me. But here I am, still waiting. (I've been working and hustling with self-employment through Woodworking and helping Authors at Story-Builds.com, but it is tough!) Sometimes I feel like Moses, that I'll never see the promised land, despite how hard I've worked and hoped.

However, I will see heaven, and nothing compares to that!

- Last month, my work truck broke down and still isn't fixed.
- Last week, my daily driver broke down, after I had just spent nearly a thousand dollars on new tires and wheels (long story, but I was nursing those old tires for MONTHS to make them last!).
- My windshield cracked all the way across during the only snow this year.
- Had to replace the alternator... myself. Did I mention money was tight? Tighter than tight, tighter than Spanx, so I hear.
- In between the breakdowns (not to mention other breakdowns), my wife got sick, our oldest got the flu TWICE, our ten-month-old baby was fighting some stuff as well, I was on and off with sinus/throat junk—all within three weeks. I was unable to work much during those times, and I don't get paid unless I'm producing content or furniture, and not even then sometimes.
- Sleepless nights, lots of doctor visits, paying out the... for meds

- Hmm, what else? My laptop was blown off a stand during an outdoor gig, but it survived, a little more battle-worn and scarred, just like us.
- One of the most painful fights with my wife in our 9 years of marriage, just one night after we tried praying together (another story for another time).

Stay with me here! I'm actually an optimist, sometimes. The truth is, I'm leaving a lot out. It's not because I want to limit the 'side effects' list of following Jesus, but it's because I'm truly finding a way to rejoice in our tribulations. At this point, I don't think I could make a full list of things that are going 'wrong' (from my limited perspective). I'm choosing to keep my eyes fixed ahead.

One thing I'll add here: things going wrong don't bother me as much now. I've been hearing the phrase, "roll with the punches," lately, and I get it. If you get knocked out, you're not very useful.

I believe God wants me to be tougher and softer at the same time, holy with higher capacity.

I trust that God is using these things to grow me and prepare me for greater things, both greater in suffering and greater in joy. One powerful verse I cling to in times like this is Romans 8:28 (who knew Romans was such a powerful book about hope?!).

> We know that all things work together for the good of those who love God, who are called according to his purpose."
> -Romans 8:28, CSB

Notice the future tense of all of these Scripture sections. That is where I'm keeping my focus. That is the secret to hope, and honestly, to survival.

I like to paraphrase a powerful statement which I believe stems from Lysa Terkheurst, "Disappointment is His appointment."

I write books, non-fiction like this, and fiction. I believe in the power of story and storytelling.

Not only is hope one of the most powerful things offered by God, but it is also my driving theme in my upcoming fiction series, "Luminant," where a teenager's parents go missing, but he hasn't lost hope that they are still alive. It gets a little sci-fi and a lot fantastic, but he discovers lands under the earth. He learns that he has to go deep to learn the truth, and the more he uncovers, the more hope he must hold to and call upon. Luka hears about Romans 5 from his grandmother, but it isn't until he is truly tested that he learns the real power of hope.

I've had mine tested, and not just recently. I have a scar, of sorts, one that I can't hide, and it has shaped my hope. Not everyone notices, or they're polite enough to say they don't, but I don't know how. Some just think it's a lazy eye, but it's actually a prosthetic.

When I was eleven, I lost my left eye to a lawn dart. This event laid two paths in front of that little boy. I chose to trust God's sovereignty, that God allowed this to happen for a greater reason. An event that could have obliterated hope actually built it. It has shaped me in many ways, and I own it as a major part of my story. I love to laugh, and I invite humor into my potentially hopeless situation.

As many jokes as there are, I still enjoy hearing them from friends who've earned the right to jest. One of my favorites took far too long to realize: "There's only one "i" in Michael." There's the old "turn a blind eye," or "try not to get on my bad side," and the classic Bible reference, "if your eye causes you to sin..." We had a lot of fun with that one at purity conferences.

I want people to remember me not as "the guy with one eye" but as an encouraging person, one who speaks life with each breath and reflects

Christ. One of the main tools in that pursuit is hope, and it doesn't come easily. It takes work, it takes hardship, it takes faith.

Consider this enlightening perspective:

> Hope itself is like a star—not to be seen in the sunshine of prosperity and only to be discovered in the night of adversity."
> -Charles Spurgeon

Hope is not about a moment, it's about each moment. Each moment, look to Christ, who is our hope. Make your requests known, and wait patiently for God's answers and provision.

When I plead with God, I sometimes hear something like, "No." But then, "I'll do more, more than you can imagine."

> Now to Him who is able to do immeasurably more than all we ask or imagine, according to His power that is at work within us, to Him be glory in the church and in Christ Jesus throughout all generations, forever and ever! Amen."
> -Ephesians 3:20-21, NIV

When you're in the darkest of nights, stay focused on what may only be a pinprick of light coming through the keyhole, because behind that door waits immeasurably more than we can dream of.

∾

Michael Lacey is the best-selling author of *As We Fight: A Weekly Guide Through the Warfare of Worship* and the fiction series, *Luminant*. He is a Christ-follower, husband, loving father, worship leader, woodworker, and Story Builder. With his brand, Story Builds Creative, he helps authors and creatives build their stories and get their works and words into the world.

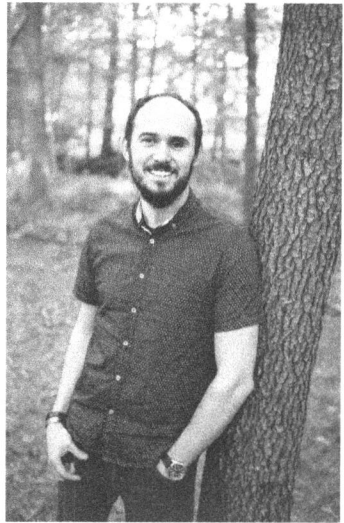

Fill out Michael's author survey at StoryBuildsCreative.com to book a free consultation/clarity session for your own writing. You can also email him at michael@ michaellacey.me for any questions concerning faith, writing, and creative pursuits.

Get both his worship devotional and audiobook for FREE, as well as the "7 Strategies to Strengthen Your Worship," at michaellacey.me/freereading.

To show your appreciation, give a physical copy to your local worship leader, grab it here: https://amzn.to/348eMf2

# IT'S AMAZING WHAT YOU CAN LIVE THROUGH BY ANGIE WALTHALL

*And he [Job] said:*
   *"Naked I came from my mother's womb,*
   *And naked shall I return there.*
   *The* LORD *gave, and the* LORD *has taken away;*
   *Blessed be the name of the* LORD.*""*
      *-Job 1:21*

*And the* LORD *said to Satan, "Behold, he is in your hand, but spare his life.""*
      *-Job 2:6*

First of all, I'm oversimplifying several long, very complicated stories to make time to get to the point. As a child I had cancer. At one point my heart stopped. Though the medical team was able to resuscitate me, they gave my family little hope for survival and much less hope for any kind of normal life. Obviously I survived, however, their predictions were far from the truth.

Fast forward about 13 years: I grew up, graduated sixth in a very large class, opened a business, got married, had kids, and the list goes on. Each and every one of those things were a miracle in and of itself. I'll take time to share the details of one of those. Well, really it's two, but you'll get the point.

Because of surgeries, and chemo, and scar tissue and cysts, I was told many times that I would not be able to have children. My husband, due to injuries from a horrendous wreck, was also told that he would not be able to have children. BUT GOD. We have two miracles, Micah (now 18) and Aaron (now 16). The delivery of Micah ended up being an emergency due to a medication error. The doctor ripped the cords out of the wall and took the whole bed to the O.R. thinking he was about to lose both of us.

After having Aaron, my doctor told me it was

not safe to have any more children, so we opted for me to have a tubal ligation along with the C-section. On the follow-up visit my doctor told us, "I'm NOT a religious person. However, there's only one way you ever had kids, because there's not enough of anything in there connected to anything else that you should ever have been able to have children."

Fast forward another six years. In the spring of 2009, after having strange dizzy spells and thinking I had an ear infection, I was diagnosed with a brain tumor. Initially the neurosurgeon said that it had the appearance of cancer on the MRI, but he wouldn't know exactly what kind until he got in there. Surgery was scheduled for late July. I really thought this one was going to take me home. I had just lost a very close friend to a brain tumor.

The day of surgery, friends and family came to the hospital with me, many stayed and waited during surgery—so many—to the point that when the surgeon came out to give a report he questioned the volume of people that answered when he called my name. My best friend said he looked like Eeyore when he came out to give the first report, still believing the worst case scenario. She said he looked like Tigger bouncing when he came out to give the second report that it was not cancer and that it was not even attached to anything but my olfactory (smelling) nerve. By the way, he removed that nerve—I shouldn't be able to smell. BUT GOD. I can smell just fine.

Fast forward three more years and I had to have yet another hernia surgery; I had already had four, including one as a child. Because of all the surgeries and scar tissue that I have, along with another issue (we found out after my brain surgery that my skin is about a quarter the normal thickness of most people), I have issues with healing and abscesses. Therefore, I have issues with muscles healing also. The first hernia I noticed was on Christmas Day after Aaron was born. Every other one, except when I was a child and a tiny one now, has been related to that one.

To finally get some more stability and be able to deal with the problem my surgeon called in a colleague to do a procedure called a component separation. In that surgery they pull muscles from your sides around to connect in the front to form another layer of muscle. It was a very painful process, and because of that and the time frame when I was in the hospital (during the doctor's family vacation) I was immobile longer than desired. In the process, I developed a pulmonary embolism—not just any pulmonary embolism, one called a saddle p.e., meaning it was large enough to block both lungs. The fact that I was still in the hospital probably saved my life yet again. BUT GOD. Not only was I still in the hospital, but a nurse's aide was in the room with me when it hit. He was able to call in the medical team immediately.

Time after time in my life I have faced so many things that should have ended in other serious health issues or death—there are many more that I could list but space doesn't allow me to list them all in detail. Here are a few more in short: fell down a flight of stairs; totaled a car; did a 360 on the interstate on ice and ended up facing backward on an off ramp; fell on a wet floor and ended up within inches of hitting my head on a metal bar; dislocated a knee and ended up in the ER to have it put back; rolled an SUV and ended up taking a helicopter ride to the MED; thirty-one surgeries to date (any one could've been the end); hepatitis C (cured by the way); chemo three times; radiation (caused the brain tumor); toxoplasmosis (could be blind); another small brain tumor; a seven year long MRSA infection; among other things; BUT GOD!!!

Yahweh, Jehovah, Elohim, Addonai, Abba, the LORD is the ONLY ONE who knows the number of our days and when it's time for us to go home. NO ONE, and I mean NO ONE, else has that privilege. It's amazing what you can live through.

He never promised us a rose garden. In fact, He warned us that we would have trouble:

> *These things I have spoken to you, that in Me you may have peace. In the world you will have tribulation; but be of good cheer, I have overcome the world."*
> *-John 16:33*

In this unprecedented time of crisis, it's easy to be swept away by the chaos and disparity that is flowing non-stop through the media. Be careful to be anxious for nothing, that the peace of God can guard your hearts and minds in Christ Jesus [a], remembering Who the Author and Finisher of our faith [b] is. Take every thought captive to the obedience of Christ [c].

Look up verses; learn them; read them out loud; pray them. The best stance you can take in times of trial is the same one Jesus took against the evil one during His time of temptation in the wilderness. He didn't argue with the devil; He didn't have a conversation with him; He simply told him what God had already said in Scripture: "It is written . . . ." (Matthew 4:4, 7, 10).

As Christ's followers, our weapons of warfare are not of this world [d], so we cannot fight as the world fights. He has already won. The devil is angry because he knows his time is short [e]. He cannot take back Christ's followers, however, he can keep us from taking others with us, if we let him.

Don't let the trials, pains, and scars of this temporary life keep you from sharing the joy that Christ has placed within you. Sing of His love forever; shout to the LORD; sing of His great faithfulness.

Let me add to my previous list of: look up verses; learn them; read them out loud; pray them. Also, be purposeful in creating the soundtrack of your life. If you will notice, almost every song you grew up listening to has a memory attached to it— some good, some bad, some horrible. Be careful what you allow yourself to listen to. I'm not saying you have to listen to all Christian music, unless that is a conviction that God has pressed upon you for some reason, as He did me. However, some songs will have a tendency to sweep us into melancholy moods, and depression, and anger because of the memories attached to them.

God gave me that conviction early on, because I went through a terrible time of depression in my early teen years, and all of the songs of that era drag me right back to those feelings. I don't only listen to Christian music, but my radio presets are only on Christian music, because I know my tendencies because God showed them to me early in my walk. Ask God to reveal weaknesses that you need to take steps to deal with. Ask for accountability.

This world is not our home; we are just passing through. We are all terminal; none of us will get out of this alive, unless Jesus comes back first. Don't live in fear. Walk in faith. Live in a way that makes others wonder what you've got and want it. Be prepared to share the reason for the hope that is within you [f] in spite of the scars that you accumulate along the way. The scars just give you a platform to share the goodness [g] of the LORD.

Prayer: LORD, teach me to glorify You, praise You at all times [h]. Show me how to use everything in my life to point others to You, even my scars. Help me to comfort others with the comfort You have comforted me [i] with. Help me to love You with all my heart, mind, soul, and strength, and love my neighbor as myself [j]. Teach me to redeem the time, LORD [k], that I may glorify You with every breath I have left.

P.S. Don't let survivor's guilt paralyze you either. It's not your choice who goes home and when, and who is left behind to keep fighting the good fight. I've had two very close friends go home from brain tumors, one before mine and one after. I can't answer why. His ways are not our ways and

His thoughts are not our thoughts [l]. It's not mine to choose and neither is it yours. Just trust Him.

FOOTNOTES: a. Philippians 4:6-7 | b. Hebrews 12:2 | c. II Corinthians 10:5 | d. v 3-4 | e. Revelation 12:12 | f. I Peter 3:15 | g. Deuteronomy 7:9; Ezra 3:11; Psalm 136 | h. Psalm 34:1 | i. II Corinthians 1:4 | j. Mark 12:30-31 | k. Ephesians 5:16 | l. Isaiah 55:8-9

~

*E*ven as a young girl, the sight of blank paper excited Angie, begging her to put something on it. Her passion for coffee and youth ministry led her to take ownership of a coffee shop, which led to a relationship, which further led Angie to tell her story in her book, *Common Ground*. It is filled with the details of how God used the coffee shop, Common Ground, to change the course of her life. Because of the convictions she received early on, she has a passion to let young people know that Godly relationships with holy boundaries are possible. There is an alternative to the world's view of "dating," and she wants to show you how to lay the groundwork and make a plan in advance to succeed. As a young child, she battled cancer, and later in life other health issues stemming from complications and the treatment of cancer. She believes God has chosen to keep her here "for such a time as this," and is determined to fulfill His will as long as He allows her to have breath. She and her husband, Andrew, live in Southaven, MS, with their two boys, Micah and Aaron. The family attends First Baptist Church Horn Lake, where she is the Women's Ministry Coordinator. She hopes to be serving in youth ministry again as soon as the LORD brings the ministry of The House to fruition—in HIS timing.

You can read Angie's blog at: https://motherof2angie.net/

Follow on Twitter and Facebook: @motherof2angie

Get Angie's book, *Common Ground,* today:

Amazon: https://amzn.to/3jlloig

Lifeway: https://www.lifeway.com/en/product/common-ground-P005639135

# TRUSTING GOD THROUGH TURMOIL AND TRAUMA BY MEREDITH SWIFT

My elder daughter Sarah is non-verbal autistic. She is a strong and energetic young woman who usually enjoys robust good health. But in 2016, Sarah was stricken with a very serious illness. It had begun with a slight cold that worsened into a chest infection and was compounded by a severe urinary tract infection. Antibiotics were prescribed and administered, and the infection seemed to clear, but Sarah would not leave her bed. I had to spoon feed her, force water into her, and drag her to the toilet. She was losing weight at an alarming rate. Admitted to hospital overnight, all tests came back negative.

As Sarah's condition worsened, so did my fear. I was terrified that my daughter was going to die.

She couldn't speak to me and tell me what was going on inside her body and mind. I felt powerless to help her and powerless to lean on God and trust Him through this storm. I was angry with Him, believing He was allowing Sarah to be so sick. I would bargain with Him, asking Him to make *me* ill, instead of Sarah. She was defenceless! It didn't seem fair at all.

Sarah's doctor believed she was depressed and prescribed antidepressants to aid in her recovery. She began taking the medication and, slowly, she did begin to get better—eating and drinking, and able to get out of bed. I believed we were heading into calmer waters. Little did I know, but things were going to take a turn for the worse.

Even though Sarah was eating, drinking, and mobile, she was now self-harming—banging her head, screaming uncontrollably, and biting her wrists – as well as attacking me and my other daughter without warning. We would regularly call the ambulance and Sarah would be given a shot to calm down. This was a time of intense pain and suffering—for all of us, and especially for Sarah, who could not vocalise what she was experiencing. I believed the medication to be the cause of Sarah's anguish, and after consulting with my doctor I decided to wean her off it. This was a long process which took months. Sarah's unpredictable self-harming and acts of violence meant that this was a debilitating and exhausting time for all of us.

I felt as though I was navigating my way through a minefield, and even though I continued to speak with and pray to Him, I felt very disconnected from Jesus. I was lying in bed one night angrily demanding that God tell me why this was all happening. No answer. Tears of anguish and frustration poured out of me. And finally, when I was spent, I remember saying "I don't know why You are doing this, but I am going to trust You".

Philippians 4:7 tells us

> And the peace of God, which passes all understanding, will keep your hearts and your minds in Christ Jesus."

At that precise moment of deciding to trust Him, I had surrendered to God, laying my heavy burden down. Instead of asking why this situation was happening, I surrendered to the fact that God knew what He was doing. I did not have to *understand* why this was happening; I just had to *trust Him*.

And at that precise moment of deciding to trust Him, all the exhaustion and stress literally slid off me, and I felt God's peace. It was not a sensation I can even begin to adequately describe, but as I drew close to God on that night, He drew close to me, enveloping me in the sweetest and purest peace I had ever known. It was the perfect peace of surrendering to the God of all creation; the One who created us and who has a good plan for our lives. I no longer felt alone like I had, disconnected from Jesus and wandering around in my own self-imposed wilderness.

I look back at that time and I see it as a turning point not only in my faith journey, but in my life—in everything that is of substance in me. It was a turning point because I came to the end of myself and I handed my situation over to God. Things did not magically improve overnight, but experiencing the totality of God's peace not only altered my perspective, it forever changed me. Seeing my daughter not only gravely ill but also witnessing her self-harming, as well as being exhausted by the unpredictability of her violence, brought me to a point where I had no alternative but to lay my heavy burden at the foot of the Cross. I simply could not find a way out and I certainly could not continue in the way I was. The process of surrendering to God was a long and slow one as I kicked and screamed like a tantruming two-year-old, trying to do everything in my own strength. But He waited faithfully as I came to the end of myself and then He stepped down and lifted me up in His loving arms, saturating me with His Holy peace and filling me with His living water.

In Matthew 11.30 Jesus tells us His yoke is easy and His burden is light. By taking His yoke we are joined to Him and we can then *allow* Him to steer us in His right direction. Remember, we have free will and we choose freely to surrender and allow Him to do what needs to be done. Then, and only then, can He work with us and fulfill in us the good plan He has for our lives.

The act of surrender is also an act of obedience. As followers of Jesus, we are called to trust God and obey Him. We are called to trust Him in *all* circumstances, through good times and bad. Can you choose to cling onto Him, no matter what you are experiencing in your life? There are some things that we will never understand this side of Heaven, and it is futile to continue to try to do so. God is on the throne. We can trust Him absolutely—for He alone is good and perfect. Jesus is the same yesterday, today and forever (Hebrews 13:8); He is faithful; our overcomer, our redeemer; our burden-bearer and our rest-giver.

## QUESTIONS FOR REFLECTION

Do you have a situation in your life where you want to know why things are happening, but God is not revealing this to you?

Can you make the choice to allow God to take charge, to leave the situation in His hands?

> For just as the heavens are higher than the earth, so are My ways higher than your ways, and My thoughts than your thoughts."
> -Isaiah 55:9

> Cast your burden on the LORD, and He shall sustain you; He shall never permit the righteous to be moved."
> -Psalm 55:22

> Trust in the LORD with all your heart, and lean not on your own understanding; 6 In all your ways acknowledge Him, and He shall direct your paths."
> -Proverbs 3:5

For God has not given us the spirit of fear; but of power, and of love, and of a sound mind."
     -2 Timothy 1:7

*All scriptures taken from New Spirit-Filled Life Bible, New King James Version.

~

I am originally a farm girl, being raised on a sheep and dairy farm in Victoria, Australia, but now I reside in the city of Townsville in beautiful, tropical Far North Queensland. Writing has always been a big part of my life – through my journals and each of my four books.

Each of my books comes from a foundation of my faith and covers an aspect of my life—struggles with drugs, alcohol, depression, domestic violence, and the challenges of raising a child with special needs. All are available on Amazon and I have been humbled and grateful to have received many great reviews and hear of lives that have been touched by my work.

Accepting Jesus into my heart and being born again has transformed my life, which had a lot of pain and sadness in it. But God has given me beauty for ashes, and He has transformed this pain and sadness through my writing. My hope is that my books give encouragement and healing, and help people know they are not alone in their pain.

Besides my love for Jesus and my family (I have two beautiful daughters) and friends, I also teach kindergarten and love to read. I also love to cook! I am a "thrower", taking ingredients and throwing them together, creating a taste sensation that is nourishing and comforting. Good coffee, my three spoiled cats and faithful Golden Retriever round out my life.

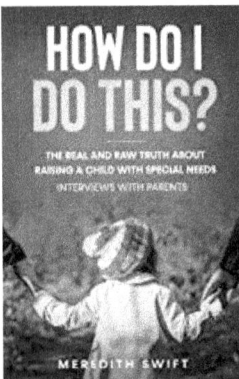

My author website is www. meredithswiftauthor.com and you can follow me on Instagram @MerryFree2015 or Facebook at https://www.facebook.com/GardenOfPromise.

Get Meredith's books today: https://amzn.to/3oon0ol

# YOU ARE GOOD ENOUGH BY MIMI EMMANUEL

*S*o You Think I'm a Lousy Friend, Do You? Shall we go for a ride? YES!

## RACING ALONG THE SHORELINE

That indescribable feeling of the sea breeze in my face and my hair. I don't think that I'll ever get enough of that. The salt on my lips, the fresh air tickling my nostrils. My daughter and best buddy by my side as we race along the shoreline. My daughter on her bike and my friend Donna next to me on her colourful recumbent trike. Yellow with a pink canopy and all kinds of colours flapping in the salty breeze. Her canine companion Cupid nestled in his basket on the back of her trike. And there we go. Lilac is running beside me. All of us grinning from ear to ear.

Soo good. Soo good!

What makes you think I'm a lousy friend?

## WE SHARED LUNCH EVERY TIME

I brought lunch every time. And I shared with you, every time. Crackers and cheese and those weird purple corn crackers with my homemade organic yoghurt dip with sweet chilli sauce. Apple strips of red capsicum, walnuts, and miso soup. I shared my shake with you also, and water. Always plenty of water because it's hot on the Fraser Coast in summer. Very hot.

You'd bring exotic guacamole dip and gluten-free crackers. Not because you were gluten intolerant but because I am.

Doesn't sound like lousy friends. Does it?

So why do I feel like one?

## WE ALWAYS AGREED ON EVERYTHING

You always wanted to talk and I always wanted to race. I need to feel life itself against my skin, and the wind, the salt, the warmth, the buzz. I feel that best at speed.

Then I'd slow down and we'd go slow together

and we'd talk. You would talk and I would agree with you. And then I'd talk and you would agree with me. We never disagreed. We both have lived long enough to know that friendships are based on what we agree on and not on differences.

I always looked forward to our get-togethers and our rides, and you told me that our gatherings were special to you too.

I shouldn't feel like a lousy friend, should I? But I do.

## WE LAUGHED A LOT

I love your quirky sense of humour and we laugh a lot. Your gentle, kind nature always finds the positive in everything and everyone. We talked about life and love and all sorts of good stuff.

It's such a pleasure to call you my friend. I never wanted our friendship to end.

I thought you felt the same.

## YOU CRAZY CAT, RIDING IN THE THUNDER

We celebrated Christmas together on the beach, December 2019. You and I and my niece and daughters and her fiancée and some lovely friends from church. It was one of my best Christmases by far. And you agreed. All of us wanted to stay there forever in the shade under the trees at the edge of our beach.

And then the thunder came and we all rushed off, and you decided to ride in the thunder, you crazy cat. But you ended up sheltering with a bunch of strangers near the esplanade under a tin roof.

And I checked up on you and made sure that you were okay.

Isn't that what good friends do? So why do I feel so lousy?

## GOAL SETTING

At our last meeting, we discussed goal setting. At the beginning of 2020, it was exciting to share our plans. I told you that I hadn't even begun my life yet. I told you that I still had so much to fit in and I shared my deep desires and plans with you. I asked you what your plans for 2020 were. And you said that you had no particular plans other than for us to do more triking together. You told me that you had lived a good life and had a lot of fun and didn't feel the need for goal setting.

As close friends, we grinned and shared intimate details of our 'past lives.'

I didn't feel like a lousy friend then. I felt like your best buddy.

## COME HOME WITH ME

My daughter was having trouble loading my trike in our car and I asked for your advice. I walked with you to your car, and you shared the best way to load the trike in the car. It is then that you shared with me once more that you were concerned about the bush fires; living in remote bushland and all that.

Both my daughter and I told you to come home with us. We said, 'Don't even bother going home. Stay with us.' You looked at me and I said, 'You know that I mean that, don't you?' And you said, 'Yes.' And my daughter reiterated the invite.

Surely you didn't think that I was a lousy friend then... did you?

## WE RETRACED OUR STEPS

My daughter and I went back there yesterday. We went back to the spot where we last met at the riverside theatre in Maryborough. We retraced our steps, and I rode my trike where we last rode together. Remember how we went through the park and over the railway line? Remember how we were going to have a cuppa at the restaurant on the river and found that it was closed? It was closed yesterday too.

I brought my new puppy, whom you never met. Her name is Mellow. And she was brilliant. She ran alongside me and when she was tired, she climbed in the cart behind my trike. Her floppy ears raised higher and higher as I sped up.

And toward the end of our ride, my trike battery died. Just like you. No warning... just died.

## WHY BOTHER

And I thought to ask the band that was playing to play a song in memory of my dear friend Donna, but then I couldn't, and didn't. Why bother? I was sitting there and just couldn't get up to ask them because...

I felt that you thought that I was a lousy friend.

## TRUE FRIENDS ARE FOREVER

I thought that we were forever friends. As I was sitting in front of the stage, pretty much in the same spot as where you and I sat a few weeks ago,

I was thinking, 'Do I want to dedicate a song to you for your sake or for myself? Or maybe for both of us? To honour our friendship? Perhaps dedicating a song to you will give me some sense of closure?'

As my tears flowed freely, I realised that it is unlikely that I will ever get closure on your departure.

Your family said that you went out on your own terms. And that you did.

I'm disagreeing with you now. I will never agree with you on your choice. I doubt that I will ever have peace about you leaving me behind the way that you did.

Because Donna, surely had I been a better friend, you wouldn't have wanted this life to end...

～

Father, help!!
I'm changing my pillow cover... again. It's 2 o'clock at night. I didn't know someone could cry that much.

'Father, are You there? I need You. I need You to know that Donna is a good person. The pastor told me that she made her choice and that's all there is to it. Did I miss something? Father, is there anything that I should have, could have done to keep Donna here? To make sure that angels would carry her straight to You? Father, what did I miss?'

'Did I miss a memo?'

'I beg Your pardon?'

'Did I miss a memo?'

I'm wiping my face. 'What memo?'

'The memo which says that Mimi Emmanuel is responsible for people staying on this earth. And the memo that says that it is Mimi's responsibility where people go after they die.'

'....'

'Did Donna ask you for help?'

'No, she didn't, Father.'

'Did you offer support?'

'Yes, I did.'

'So she chose not to accept the help you offered her. She could have reached out to you, but she chose not to. That should tell you something. I could have nudged you, but I didn't.

This wasn't between you and her. This was between her and Me.

Are you the one that keeps people alive?'

I stood corrected.

No, I am not the one that keeps people alive. My mind went back to various medical emergencies where I literally begged my Father to keep me alive for the sake of my children. And He answered my prayers. I cannot even keep myself alive without His help, let alone someone else. I was well aware of that.

I blurted out, 'I want to meet her again. She's a good sort, You need to know that. I don't care if she was a Christian or not. Who cares, what does any of that matter anyway?'

'Who says that this matters?'

'Well, You know, the churches do, and fellow Christians. As far as they're concerned, Donna is going to hell. I'm telling You, this lady had a heart that made mine and my daughter's sing in a good way.'

'When did I say that non-Christians go to hell? Didn't my Son Jesus tell you the story about the Samaritan?'

'Yep, He did, Father.'

'Then you realise that the lawyer who asked Jesus about eternal life was told that 'religion' doesn't matter. It's all about the heart and the actions that follow; as you well know.'

'I know, I know.'

'Nor is it any of your business what happens when someone else comes knocking on those pearly gates. You just worry about your own life and about not hiding your light under a basket so that no one can see it.'

'I know, I know.'

'Were you *the best you* when you were with your friend Donna?'

'I did my best, Father. I would have gone riding with her more often and hung out with her more frequently had there been the opportunity. But given my limitations and capabilities... yes, I did the best I could.'

Suddenly, my chest heaved from the big gulps of air coming in. I was breathing again.

It wasn't my fault. I hadn't done anything wrong. It wasn't between her and me.

'Next time, talk to Me first. Stay in touch more often.

Now wipe your face and get out into the world.

Be your best!'

## REFERENCES

Was I a lousy friend?—don't talk to the dead —Deuteronomy 18:10-13, Isaiah 8:19-20 | Good Samaritan story—It's about the heart and actions —Luke 10:25-37 | Our life is in your hands —Deuteronomy 10:14, Job 12:10 | It's not between us and them or the world, it's between us and the Lord—Luke 23:43 | The Lord is our judge—Isaiah 33:22 | Don't hide your light—Be your best! —Matthew 5:14-16 | Go out into the world—Mark 16:15

~

*W*ritten by Mimi in memory of my buddy, my friend, my bestie who died Jan 7, 2020.

The events are true but names and places have been changed. You can find Mimi on www.mimiemmanuel.com. Get Mimi's books on Amazon here: https://amzn.to/3iqZCqI

~

*P*hone numbers for suicide prevention and support after suicide

AUS—Lifeline 24-hour national telephone crisis counselling service 13 11 14

US—1-800-SUICIDE, 1-800-784-2433. 1-800-273-TALK, 1-800-273-8255

UK—Suicide.org—Hotline: 1850 60 90 90

# HOPE IN THE DARKNESS BY KELLY WALK HINES

When I was just three years old, my mother was murdered by her boyfriend. I am the youngest of five children who were left unintentionally abandoned. This was just the beginning of a chaotic, heartbreaking time that I would call my childhood. We moved from the home with our mother in Florida to New Jersey to live with people who were practically strangers. My dad was awarded custody of me when I was six. At this point, I had only met him a handful of times. He was practically a stranger. My dad had remarried and had a stepson that was just a few months older than me. I was forcibly removed from my siblings in favor of this new family. The judge ruled that "any trauma Kelly would endure by moving away from her siblings would be countered by the stability of a home with two parents." Unfortunately, that couldn't have been further from what happened.

Alcohol and drugs shaped the way my dad handled things. He was very angry and paranoid. He would scream at us all. He was violent to my stepmom and step-brother mostly. I was spared a lot of the physical pain because I learned to become invisible to protect myself. I figured you couldn't hurt what you couldn't see. I was a very sad and scared little girl. When others were playing pretend, learning how to put on makeup, and forging valuable friendships, I was trying to survive in the turbulent place I called home. I finally moved out at twenty-one with the clothes on my back and my nursing books. I remember running through the woods in the dead of winter, following the moonlight peeking through the trees. I would not return for another year to get some of my things. I was finally free.

Truth is, although I would not want to live it again, I learned to see the light of hope shining within the darkness. A lifeline in the midst of troubles. I found God at a young age and even though I didn't understand it completely, I knew that Jesus loved me. Faith saved me and continues to save me. Hope is the action of faith and what I rely on in the stressful times in my life. I learned to be thankful for my tough childhood. I have used my past to make me stronger. I would not be who I am today, I would not be able to help people going through their own tough times, without my past. I learned to give others a home because I was abandoned. I taught others how to grieve because of all the losses I had been through. I grew up without a mom so I had the drive to be the best one I could be. Because of my sadness, I could help others learn to find hope. Because I grew up with family violence and their drug use, I raised my family with love and substance-free. Through neglect, I learned the depths of love. I love that I feel emotion. I learned to transform my stubbornness into perseverance. With hard work and hope for a better tomorrow, I broke the cycle of dysfunction.

Tough times teach us lessons if we don't let it destroy our future. Some kids are born into royalty and some are born to drug-addicted parents. It's important to remember the world is not a level playing board!

Ever feel like everything is out of control? Sometimes I am stopped right in my tracks with the overwhelming weight of anxiety and stress. It feels like someone has thrown an anchor overboard. Sometimes I don't even know why, it takes me a day or two to even figure out what this weight is that I am carrying! I think of it like stones in a backpack, placed in one at a time over the course of days, months, even years. You don't even realize the gradual change until suddenly, you can't even budge. The weight is too much to even focus on anything else. On days like this, what I am learning to do is first identify the heaviness in my heart and take those rocks out, one at a time. You can't cope with your stress until you have figured out why you are stressed. Even then, the healing takes time. Just as it took time to put those rocks in your backpack, it takes time to find them and take them out.

While you cannot control what happens in your life, you are in full control of how you react and what you do next. It is incredibly empowering and incredibly true! Don't give this special power to someone else. No one else is in charge of your destiny. This is your life, grab a hold of it! Instead of letting the wind sweep you away, learn to adjust your sails and force it to move you forward. One way or another, you will get through it. You will be okay as long as you remember this: You are in control, you matter, and you are worth the work it takes to make it through.

Many days, we miss magical moments in time because we are just trying to speed through. If we aren't careful, we easily become complacent in the everyday. Wake up, work, pay bills, clean, sleep, just to repeat it all again tomorrow. I invite you to stop for just a moment, take a minute, and really look at those everyday moments. You can see the blessings around you, the little special times of ordinary life.

Look around, appreciate what you have in your life and who you have with you. If it's not what you want, change things. It's great to have goals and work toward change, it's a part of life. Without change, we simply cannot grow. It is incredibly important to realize that you are worth the change. Look at how hard you have worked for what you have. Notice the important events in your life that helped you become you. Even as a work in progress, you are enough.

Don't let people look down on you. Don't worry about people talking, they will always have something to say. The only opinions you need to worry about are yours and those of the people you hold dear. You need to love and trust yourself. When you have these two important things, you handle things differently. You will find that you can face stressful situations head-on once you have faith, a team supporting you, and a newfound belief in your own abilities. It sounds cliché, but there's a reason for that. It really, truly works!

I also encourage you to think of what your legacy will be. My legacy is being a mental health nurse and the impact I have had on the patients on the oncology unit and inpatient mental health crisis unit for kids. Of course, I loved my beautiful girls and their babies at my job, and the kids I have watched grow in my church through working with the youth group.

My legacy is also my book, *Memoirs of an Invisible Child*. Above all else, I want to give the gift of HOPE. I try to convey it with my exhibit "Hope in the Darkness: A Domestic Violence Awareness Exhibit" and my work as an advocate. I love to empower people to find their true worth and give them hope.

But I realized the legacy that blesses me the most is that my children are carrying on my mission and making it theirs. They are advocates and social activists. They help strangers and others break the cycle of dysfunction, and know their own, profound value. The next generation of our family will even be stronger and healthier than us, can you imagine the change they will make? It just makes me so happy and thankful for that wonderful gift! I pray my grandkids and generations to come will continue that legacy.

When people tell me that they love my kids and when I hear stories of the kind things they have done, it just makes whatever battles I overcame to get here feel worth it. I am so very blessed! I challenge you to think of your legacy. What do you strive to bring to the table? I pray you always find Hope in the Darkness.

~

My name is Kelly Walk Hines, and I reside in New Jersey. I am a 48-year-old divorced Christian mother of two wonderful adult children. I am currently dating a wonderful, kind man who has a great son. I am very happy and blessed.

I have been a registered nurse since 1992. I specialize in mental health nursing. I fix people from the inside out. I spent about ten years working at an inpatient crisis mental health unit for children and adolescents. I spent another ten years working with pregnant and parenting teens. Both jobs were such blessings.

I am proud of my life's work. God took the trauma of my past and used it to help me relate to others and help them find healing. I am currently working on my second book, and I look forward to many more years of writing. I am currently working on my next book that explains how I navigated through my adult life with the scars from the past. I will also be explaining my relationship with my dad as I became an adult and mother. Follow my journey on my blog on Facebook! https://m.facebook.com/invisiblechild18

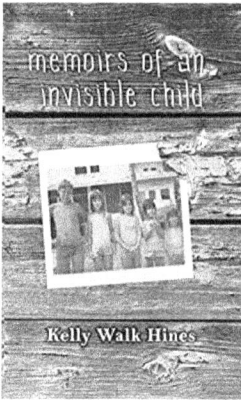

Thank you for reading my works. Any input or thoughts, please email me, memoirsofanin visiblechild@gmail.com.

www.feelinghopeful.com

Get her book today:

*Memoirs of an Invisible Child* | https://amzn.to/3n6j6nS

# REAL BIBLICAL HOPE BY MATTHEW KING

When I reflect on the word hope my mind first goes to the thought that the word hope has been cheapened in our society. When we use the word we say things like, "I hope I can do so and so," or, "hopefully that will happen in the future...". It's somewhat like the word "love." We can range from saying we love God and our wife to in the next sentence saying we love pizza and our favorite sports teams! When one word can have such a wide range of meanings it can be easy for those ranges to get closer and closer together till they become somewhat indistinguishable and lose their power. Where this really impacts our Christian walk is when we allow our day-to-day meaning of "hope" to change our Biblical understanding of the word hope. For example, when we say something like, "I hope to make it to heaven," do we mean the watered down hope we have of being able to go on a vacation this year if we save enough money? Or do we use that word with the power the Scripture uses it? This begs the question then, when we read the word "hope" in the Bible, what is it talking about?

The Biblical meaning of hope has been described as a confident expectation. I really like that description and I think you will find this to be an accurate representation after you do your own word study of this word in your Bible. But let's go ahead and dig into it a little bit here. One of my favorite passages is Lamentations 3:21-14, which says eloquently,

> *But this I call to mind, and therefore I have hope: The steadfast love of the Lord never ceases; his mercies never come to an end; they are new every morning; great is your faithfulness. 'The Lord is my portion,' says my soul, 'therefore I will hope in him.'"*

Another passage that confirms this point is in Romans 15:4, which states,

> *For whatever was written in former days was written for our instruction, that through endurance and through the encouragement of the Scriptures we might have hope."*

Paul is saying here that the Old Testament, the law, the prophets, all of it was preserved for us so that we can build up our confident expectation in the promises of God. We can trust what God has promised us is true! We don't just have to wish, we can have real unabashed confidence that God's promises to us are the truth!

Now that we see that Biblical hope is a confident expectation as opposed to the way we usually use hope as a wish, then we next need to establish what the basis of this hope is and what we can confidently expect. There is a song we sing in church called, "On Christ the Solid Rock". A key phrase for our purposes goes like this, *"My hope is built on nothing less than Jesus' blood and righteousness, I dare not trust the sweetest frame but wholly lean on Jesus' name."* Another passage from the same song goes, *"His oath, His covenant, His blood supports me in the 'whelming flood. When all around my soul gives way He then is all my hope and stay."* The meaning this song conveys is that the foundation of our hope has to be Jesus Christ and none other. Think about this passage for a minute... Titus 1:1-4 says,

> *...for the sake of the faith of God's elect and their knowledge of the truth, which accords with godliness, in hope of eternal life, which God, who never lies, promised before the ages began and at the proper time manifested in his word through the preaching with which I have been entrusted by the command of God our Savior."*

Did you hear that!? God, Who is absolute truth (that's why this hope is a confident expectation), had this plan of eternal life for us before the world even began! To be honest, that kind of blows my mind and I have to take a break thinking about it because I don't totally understand how that works. But here is what I do know... God is unchangeable, He loves me, He gave up His Son for me, and if He has had this plan of me being able to spend eternity with Him since before the world even began, then I can trust that He will fulfill His Word and if I obey Him I can lay hold of that promise.

A Christians hope is different from the world's

hope. Look at 1 Timothy 6:17-19 for a moment. The Apostle Paul says,

> *As for the rich in this present age, charge them not to be haughty, nor to set their hopes on the uncertainty of riches, but on God, who richly provides us with everything to enjoy. They are to do good, to be rich in good works, to be generous and ready to share, thus storing up treasure for themselves as a good foundation for the future, so that they may take hold of that which is truly life."*

Here Paul shows that those who are materially focused have their confidence (or hope) in their wealth, while a Christians hope must be firmly in what is "truly life." Contrast this with another of Paul's messages in 1 Corinthians 15:19 where he states,

> *If in Christ we have hope in this life only, we are of all people most to be pitied."*

He goes on to talk about what that future hope looks like, but the point I want to make here is that if our hope is only about what God can do for us in this life, then it isn't really the hope talked about in the Bible. It is just like the rich people Paul talked about in 1 Timothy, and that's not the example we want to emulate. Paul is saying that the Christian's ultimate hope is in the eternal life Jesus has promised us if we follow His Word. This is the hope we have that will not disappoint and that we can confidently expect.

So, practically speaking, what does this mean for us? How does having this hope change my life on a day-to-day basis? I think there are several things we can take away from what we have learned so far and apply to our lives. Let's see...

1. **Our Doubts Should Be Reduced.** I don't know about you, but depending on how you were raised and what churches you attended, this might be different. At least for me, growing up I heard a lot of Christians doubt their salvation. They had been saved, they lived the best lives they could, and they followed God as best they knew how, but they still felt like it was a 50/50 shot once they got to the pearly gates. This isn't what God wanted or expected of His Children.

2. **We Still Have To Live Right.** Despite God's promise of salvation He still expects us to live within the parameters He has set for us in His Word. This takes daily dedication and discipline. Check out Titus 2:11-15 where Paul says,

> *For the grace of God has appeared, bringing salvation for all people, training us to renounce ungodliness and worldly passions, and to live self-controlled, upright, and godly lives in the present age, waiting for our blessed hope, the appearing of the glory of our great God and Savior Jesus Christ, who gave Himself for us to redeem us from all lawlessness and to purify for Himself a people for His own possession who are zealous for good works. Declare these things; exhort and rebuke with all authority. Let no one disregard you."*

Jesus is always at the door knocking and wanting to come into our lives. We are the only ones who can choose to shut Him out. We can never forget that we show we love God by being obedient to Him.

**3. The World Needs Us To Share This Hope.** The world is a negative place. Maybe it always has been, but the fact is people need hope. People are searching for hope and finding artificial replacements instead of the hope we have through salvation in Christ. It is our job to share with them authentic hope through how we live our lives and by lovingly presenting them with the good news of the gospel! Now is not the time to shrink back or be timid. God has given us the spirit of power, not fear!

**4. We Should Live With Joy.** If you'll allow me a moment of honesty, this has been one of my biggest struggles as a Christian. I don't know why, but I have always struggled with being negative, with veering toward the side of pessimism and bitterness. I have battled with it most of my life, I would say, particularly the last 20 years. But I don't think that is the life God wants His children to live! He wants us to live with joy regardless of the circumstances we find ourselves in. Paul speaks of his ability to be content with situations from shipwreck and imprisonment to when he had all the physical comforts he could want. If he could be content and joyful, can't I? The answer, of course, is, "Yes!" We can be joyful in any circumstance because no matter how our lives play out God's got our backs. We have the hope and confidence of heaven. We will live eternally with those saints who have gone on before us and we will be able to commune with Jesus and our Father eternally. This fact alone should breathe joy into our lives each day, and that joy will attract those in the world to God's message who are starving for the authentic joy only God can provide.

So, what shall we say then? Hope propels us forward in our lives. It gives us meaning and a reason to press on, to persevere despite the most dire circumstances. It lets us know that everything WILL be okay in the end. I would encourage you to read through the Scriptures, looking at passages that talk about hope. Let them breathe confidence into your life so you can take hold of the life you have been called to. As the Hebrew writer says,

> *Let us hold fast the confession of our hope without wavering, for He who promised is faithful."*

Do not waver, be bold and hopeful in your faith, and God will be right beside you no matter what life brings your way.

∾

Matt King grew up as the son of a preacher in Southeastern Tennessee. His love of reading began at an early age from the nightly bedtime stories his parents read him, his older sister, and younger brother. As Matt grew up, he was inspired by his grandparents' small business to one day have a business of his own. Because of his desire to learn more about business, he received his Bachelor of Science in Business Administration from Florida College and his Master's in Management from Indiana Tech. Matt has been married to his high school sweetheart for nearly 10 years. She is an inspiration and sounding board to him and is a constant supporter. They currently live in Tampa, Florida with their Shiba Inu, Xan. Matt has written two books that are available on Amazon and has a personal development podcast called, "The Matt King Podcast" available on iTunes.

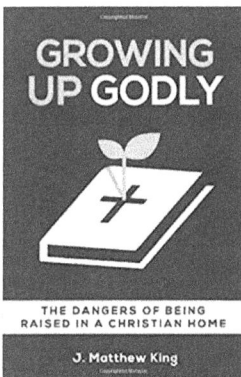

To find out about Matt's other offerings, check out his website at the link below, which has access to his books, podcast, and coaching programs. Website: https://jmatthewking. weebly.com/

. . .

Get Matt's book on Amazon:
Growing Up Godly | https://amzn.to/3l3VjmN

# WALKING WITH GOD BY KATHRYN SPRINGMAN

Susie would tell you until the day that she passed in 2007, at 90 years old, that she had a good life. Oh. Sure. It was difficult at times. "But who out of those who roam this earth have a perfect life?" she would say. Susie definitely was one to talk about the good things in her life, but if you were able to get her to talk about the hard times, she would always begin or end it with, "God always takes care of us." Very rarely did Susie ever say a bad word about anyone. Rarely did she anger, but if she did, she was kind in expressing what she had anger over. Rarely did she raise her voice. Always loving, she was an advocate for those around her.

## BOUNDARIES

Susie understood boundaries early. Before any books were written on the topic, she talked lovingly of her husband with whom she farmed the land. They were financially successful enough that they had farm hands to help. While they were in the field, she would see to the noon-time dinner meal to sustain them through the rest of the day. When it was done, she was back out in the field with them.

One day, Susie and her husband were going to have company over for the evening supper meal in their 2-room house, which consisted of a kitchen and living room. As her husband was changing his clothes, he dropped his pants and underwear by a chair. While Susie was fixing the meal, she noticed the clothes and mentioned, "You might want to pick those up." Well, he didn't. And you guessed it. Company showed up at the door and there were his dirty clothes, underwear on top, right there for everyone to see.

Aghast, he quickly picked them up. At the end of the evening after everyone left, he said to her, "I would be ashamed if I were you!" To which she answered, "Why? They weren't my clothes." He never left his clothes on the floor again.

Some of you may also be aghast, maybe for

different reasons. Maybe you think, like her husband did, that it was her job to clean up. Maybe you think like Susie, that she put in a full day of farming and was busy trying to get supper on the table and only had so much time to do it.

Once more boundaries were tested. Her daughter, Ellen, was in college about an hour away. She was rarely allowed to date. The college had a strict curfew of 8pm. Ellen felt harassed by a young man who dogged her every step asking her for a date. She finally thought, "If I go out with him and am as rude as possible, then he will leave me alone!" With that plan in place, at the end of the "date," the young man dropped Ellen off at the steps of her dormitory. Waiting on the steps were Ellen's mother Susie, Ellen's father, and her 8-year-old brother, Lee. Her father stormed down the steps and said, "I'll see you this weekend." Mortified, Ellen hugged her mother, tried to explain the situation. Susie smiled and said she would pick Ellen up on Friday.

When Friday came, Ellen got into the pickup with Susie and said, "Mom, I don't want to go home." Susie answered with a smile in her voice saying, "Oh, don't worry. There's no problem." Ellen was confused. "He was really mad. I'm in so much trouble."

"No." Susie answered. "See, I told him that you

were a young lady, an adult, capable of responsible behavior. But I told him that if he thought that was incorrect, then I would move into the dorm with you and let him and Lee run the farm. Suddenly, he realized that you were indeed a young lady, an adult, capable of responsible behavior." Susie showed everyone that she trusted that when you raise a child up in the way they should go, they will not depart from it. She trusted that. She trusted her daughter. She trusted her Savior.

## TEST OF FAITH

Susie's test of faith came in her forties. Her husband had been having digestive issues and pain after eating. His doctor said he needed to have his gall bladder out, but he refused. Finally, unable to endure the pain any longer, he decided to have his gall bladder removed.

The surgeon came out and told Susie that it was not good. Her husband's gall bladder had ruptured and turned gangrenous. As the doctor left, she said, "Lord, I know You have a bigger plan. I know that no matter what, You will take care of us."

When her husband passed not long after, Susie found herself a widow with a 20-year-old daughter still in college and a 10-year-old son at home and a farm to run. Every day, she prayed for guidance, and every day, she received it.

Two years later, Susie went back to college so she could teach school. In the midst of the hard work of being an adult student and single mother with a farm that no longer could afford farm hands, she managed her family, her studies, and her farm. She became what everyone knew she was all along: A great teacher with a gift not only of sharing knowledge, but of sharing faith.

## LESSONS FROM NATURE

Who are God's creatures? Are they not all around us? The grass that feeds the cows and horses. The crops and the fish from the pond that feed people. The birds that feed our longing for music and joy. The water that tinkles in the creek, letting us know that life moves and flows around us.

One year, when it was time to plant her crops, her brothers and nephews noticed that Susie had not gotten her fields plowed nor her crops planted. "Susie, when are you going to plant? It's getting on late in the season."

"There is a bird nest in my plow," she said.

"Move the nest. You have to get your crops planted."

"There are eggs in the nest. If I move the nest,

the mother will abandon the eggs. Are they not God's creatures? I can't in good conscience move the nest until the babies are gone."

"But Susie, you will have no crop and no money."

"God has ALWAYS taken care of me. He has always provided food in my belly and a roof over my head. He has been with me all my life and even more so since my husband died. He will care for me as He cares for the birds.

Never had her family really understood the depth of her faith and her love for all God's creatures. Her brothers worked together to quickly get their fields plowed and planted and came over with their equipment to make sure that hers were too. She did not ask her brothers to do this. She knew they had their own families and farms to take care of. But she knew with an unwavering faith that God would provide for her, as she had witnessed time and again.

## WHAT ABOUT YOU?

Susie taught us all about boundaries and faith and respect for all things God made. She respected herself enough to be completely, authentically who she was. What you saw in Susie is what you got. She wore no mask to hide her true nature. She embodied, "Love your neighbor in the same manner you love yourself." She loved herself enough to set healthy boundaries. She loved others with the same respect she gave herself. In the manner of farming and sowing and reaping, Susie received back from others what she gave: love, compassion, and respect.

Where are you today in your life and faith? Where are you in your love for yourself? Can you receive the love that is yours from your Creator? Can you love yourself enough to love others? Can you love others enough to love God? Can you love God enough to let Him love you?

No matter where you are today no matter what is happening in your life, one thing is true: God will take care of you. If we have not because we ask not, then all you have to do is ask. Then you can receive.

## PRAYER

May the God of all creation grant your wishes and prayers. Pray well. Pray the Word. Find the thing you want in Scripture and pray for that. Then you know that He will answer. My prayer for you is that God shows you His nature and His will for you. My prayer is that you come to a place where you can ask anything and know that even if you think the answer is no, there is a better plan that you will like better. You just have to ask.

## SCRIPTURE REFLECTION

> Train up a child in the way he should go, and when he is old he will not depart from it."
> -Proverbs 22:6

> Until now you have asked nothing in My name. Ask, and you will receive, that your joy may be full."
> -John 16:24

> ...you do not have because you do not ask."
> -James 4:2d

> ...but you shall love your neighbor as yourself: I am the LORD."
> -Leviticus 19:18b (The word "as" means "in the same manner.")

> Beloved, I pray that you may prosper in all things and be in health, just as your soul prospers. God takes care of the birds of the air."

-3 John 1:2

Therefore I say to you, do not worry about your life, what you will eat or what you will drink; nor about your body, what you will put on. Is not life more than food and the body more than clothing? Look at the birds of the air, for they neither sow nor reap nor gather into barns; yet your heavenly Father feeds them. Are you not of more value than they? Which of you by worrying can add one cubit to his stature?"
    -Matthew 6:25-27

Fathers, do not provoke your children, lest they become discouraged."
    -Colossians 3:21

For I know the thoughts that I think toward you, says the LORD, thoughts of peace and not of evil, to give you a future and a hope."
    -Jeremiah 29:11

All Scripture references taken from New King James Version using BibleHub.com

~

Kathryn Springman is a published author, board certified naturopathic doctor, and founder/instructor of the Sacred Space Method™. She is a certified Accunect™ practitioner and instructor, and a former BodyTalk practitioner/trainer. With over 35 years' experience in prayer, intercession, and spiritual warfare, she continues to develop and expand her knowledge and techniques. Kathryn delights in bringing to others new insights based on science combined with the ancient wisdom of God. Ms. Springman's approach to health is one that balances all aspects of our being: physical, emotional, mental, and spiritual.

Get her book, *The God Session*, today: https://amzn.to/3cPaVYd

# FROM TRAUMA TO HOPE BY JILL ROGERS

*t* all started one night when I was twenty-three years old in a relatively new marriage. I wasn't feeling well, so my husband went off to play volleyball alone. Then my good friend and neighbor called to ask me to watch her young son as she was called away in an emergency.

My first response was, "No, I don't feel well at all," but since she had no one else to help her, I agreed. Unaware that I was not alone, I walked over to the friend's house. Looming in the darkness, there was a pair of eyes watching me. After everyone was gone a man knocked on the door and asked for Mike. I told him that no Mike lived there and he uneventfully left.

After I put the child to bed, the dog was

accidentally shut in the back room, and I sat down to watch a movie. Time ticked by and my husband called to say that he would be over after the news. I was oblivious to the pair of eyes watching me through the window. I discovered later that the shadowy stranger had stacked concrete blocks to peer at me all evening long.

I assumed the knock at the door was my husband, but I was wrong. I opened the door to a strange man standing in the darkness ready to thrust in. With a swift move, there was a knife at my throat. You cannot imagine the helpless trapped feeling that you have when something like that happens to you.

I cannot begin to remember all that I said to reason with him, but I did say that the people that lived there would soon be returning, and if he left right then I would not say a word about what he'd done... but to no avail. So, I started praying for God to let me live. I told Him that night that I would do whatever He wanted me to do on this earth if I could live. It is amazing what one can do in such a short amount of time. From then on, I believe God took my life over. I cannot tell you everything was okay for me at that time, but I can tell you the way I thought about life had shifted.

I got up the next morning to go to work and went outside and the grass was greener, the birds sang clearer, and I knew I was spared for a divine purpose. That was almost forty years ago, and I lived to tell you the things that came about and how I learned to think about them.

When I went into work the next day I shared with a couple of people I worked with what had happened. One asked if I was okay and another asked if I would mind talking with someone from the Rape Crisis Center. I agreed, so she called me and we met. I was shown a photo album to see if the man was any of the possible usual suspects, and I found him there on the page looking back at me. She said the police thought that was who it might have been because he was just out of prison and was in that town.

As is the routine, I had to go pick him out of a line up at the police station. My neighbor friend, in whose house it happened, accompanied me as a witness, since she saw him as she was driving away. Later, after identifying the man, my friend and I were warned by the police that I could be in danger as a witness against him. I really didn't care at this point because I didn't want him to do this to anyone else.

I would say that when I started turning to God, it caused a wedge between my husband and me. From this experience and my prayer, I believe I received a supernatural grace and faith to cope in a new realm from here on out in my life. I had to look at everything I was going through as if getting a college education. I was going through this, learning many things along the way.

> *Where no counsel is, the people fall, but in the multitude of counsellors there is safety.*
>   -Proverbs 11:14

I got help in many ways and it took some time. But little by little, my life has come along to the place where my husband and I are helping others get healed from hurts and trauma in their lives. I got healed from the memories of it and even got my voice restored. We can never be hopeless about anything that happens to us when we pray and bring God on the scene.

I did go through several traumas in a row, including divorce, and my parents that had been married forty-four years got divorced within a short time of mine. My life seemed quite similar to Job's life for a time, but I have to say that **every bit of it** has been restored and redeemed. Sometimes we just have to trust our Heavenly Father and keep on going until we finally get to the other side. I know that if I hadn't walked through these things I would not have ever had the compassion, understanding, or wisdom to help others go through the hard things that we've helped them walk through.

> *And we know that all things work together for good to those that love God, to those who are called according to His purpose.*
> *-Romans 8:28*

Remember, anything is possible. We can never stop believing. Sometimes it's our own expectations and faith that can actually make an impossible situation become possible.

Never give up... ever.

∼

Jill has been trained in ministry and has received training through Restoring the Foundations Ministry along with Communion With God Ministries, Dr. Mark Virkler.

She and her husband have attended recovery meetings for decades to keep working on their own healing and restoration along with helping others.

They regularly attend Velocity Church,

Duquoin, IL They have always believed in living a life of accountability.

Jill offers a non-judgmental approach to getting your past healed and gaining the freedom to enjoy the present in your life.

pier7restorations.com

Jillspier7@gmail.com

Jillsblogspot

Get Jill's books today: *Shift Happens: Turning Your Stumbling Blocks to Stepping Stones* | *Stepping Stones Devotional* | *Restored to Bloom* | https://amzn.to/3nifSoO

# HOPE IN THE WAITING BY MIRANDA J. CHIVERS

*For I, the LORD your God, hold your right hand; it is I who say to you, "Fear not, I am the one who helps you." Isaiah 41:13*

In 2002, a health crisis changed my life forever. After two years of riding the medical merry-go-round with chronic unrelenting pain and fatigue, I was frustrated, angry, and exhausted. As the swelling increased around my neck, I struggled to breathe, and my voice croaked.

Initially, my family doctor dismissed my complaints, contributing the symptoms to hormonal fluctuations from menopause, a virus or just stress. Multiple prescriptions provided no relief. I persisted. When repeated blood work showed inflammation and abnormal cell counts, my doctor fumbled for answers and referred me elsewhere. The first two specialists shrugged their shoulders. A third request to a different discipline brought a flicker of hope.

Discouraged and depressed, I begged God for a solution but didn't really expect one. I felt invalidated and victimized by the medical roundabout and betrayed by my body. Fear portrayed itself through uncontrolled anger, anxiety and panic. My life was falling apart. What could God do for me?

As a busy tourist operator, social worker, and caregiver of two adult special needs daughters and a husband who traveled for a living, I had no time to be sick. This annoyance was impeding my energy and impacting my mental health and relationships. I was hanging on by a thread.

The new specialist ordered more tests to investigate my enlarged lymph glands and the odd lump under my chin. His face displayed a sympathetic gaze as he reviewed the results of the blood tests and the ultrasound. The picture was concerning, he said, cancer was a probable diagnosis. He scheduled a tissue biopsy.

We mentally prepared ourselves. On Mother's Day, we cautiously disclosed our worries over the dinner table to our adult children, encouraging them to think positive thoughts. They asked if I was dying. I said I didn't think so, but I didn't know yet. Their reassuring hugs gave me hope.

On May 29th, the surgeon sat with my husband outside the operating room, "I've been digging for two hours and I can't find the end. It's everywhere. I'm ninety-nine percent sure it's lymphoma. I've seen this before. You need to go home and prepare your family."

"How long do I have?" I asked when he broke the news to me an hour later.

"Not long. Maybe a few months. We'll know more when the biopsy results come in."

Devastated, my husband and I drove home in silence. The entire situation felt surreal—like I was living a role in a movie. I kept pinching myself. Although I knew I was very ill, I didn't feel like I was dying.

The next day, we began brainstorming how best to prepare for the worst-case scenarios. We updated our kids. I took a deep breath before calling my parents.

I was their only daughter, and they lived two thousand kilometers away. How would they handle this? I worried needlessly. Their sympathy and support were overwhelming.

They asked, "can we pray for you?"

"Sure," I replied, "it can't hurt." But I doubted it would help.

They called me almost every day, checking on my mental and physical well-being, and encouraged me to pray and read my Bible. Since they assumed I still owned one, I didn't tell them I lost the childhood gift years ago. Nor did I tell them about my recent struggle with depression that motivated me to buy a new one. I was just glad I had it.

I cracked the spine of my fresh book and reflected, "what if I die? Is this all there is?"

It wasn't the first time I'd asked myself those questions. Twice I'd suffered near-fatal car accidents. Life had smacked me around in other ways more times than I could count. Accustomed to pain and suffering and living with uncertainty, I saw trauma as a familiar villain that shadowed me like a curse. But for the past five years, life had been good.

A decade earlier, I abandoned my faith during the split with my first husband. As far as I could tell, God had done nothing for me. In fact, I blamed him for my countless tragedies. What loving God allowed a relentless stream of crises? Yet somehow, this sickness was unparalleled. For the first time, there was no explanation for the cause, no one to blame, and no luck to laugh at. It was possible that I was facing the scariest silent killer and there was nothing I could do about it.

The words, "can we pray for you?" haunted my nights.

The doctor's two-week vacation stretched the timeline for receipt of the final results to three. I crossed the days off on the calendar and pondered my bleak future.

Laughter disappeared as our somber conversations filled with anxiety. Decisions weighed. We continued business as usual — running our small cottage resort and caregiving while my husband disappeared for days, commuting for his job as an airline pilot. Worn down by unrelenting pain and fatigue, I knew I couldn't continue the hectic pace even if the diagnosis was different. Something had to give. I considered my options and resigned from my part-time social work practice.

Humiliated by my inability to control my life, I quit scoffing at God and admitted I needed supernatural help. One day, I prayed, "Dear Lord, I give up. If this is how it ends, then at least give me the grace to endure and the time to make whatever decisions are necessary."

While the waiting dragged on, the tourist season arrived in full swing. I busied myself with the administrative details and hired additional summer cleaning staff to handle the heavy, physical work. Then, in the middle of this crazy time, I doubled over in pain from a gallbladder attack. Concerned by the spiraling numbers on the blood work, my family doctor suggested waiting with surgery until the biopsy results arrived. With another brick added to my pile, I felt everything was about to topple over.

I couldn't go on. We discussed our options and then listed the business for sale. The disappointment weighed heavily. Originally, this was to be our retirement project. Over the past five years, we poured all our resources into this run-down cottage resort to fix it up and make it profitable. This was the first year the balance sheet would be more black than red. It seemed as if we were taking all our hard work and throwing it in the garbage. But what else could we do?

Financially, I didn't need to work as Ron's income could pay the bills. Yet, we couldn't shut the business down in the middle of summer. Our customers had booked their vacations and contracted staff must be paid. I grit my teeth against the unrelenting pain and held my fear at bay while we forged ahead, adjusting where we could. Ron reorganized his vacation time to span the bulk of the summer and oversaw the groundskeeping, maintenance, and cleaning staff while I shortened my office hours and took frequent rest breaks.

Parenting our adult special needs daughters added another dilemma. (My husband's daughter has Down's Syndrome and my daughter is autistic.) They needed attention and support that we could no longer provide. I researched our options, evaluated the finances, and contacted government agencies to help the girls enter independent living.

I'm still amazed at how quickly our life changed. Within weeks, an eager buyer jumped in with an offer, our daughters settled into their new home, and we were shopping for ours.

Reflecting, I'm convinced that whenever we step out in faith, we open the door for God to move. A friend said, "God never goes where he's not welcome. When we invite him, he comes in and starts cleaning house." I realized he was renovating ours.

I prayed for a miracle and the grace to handle the next phase. Regardless of the diagnosis, I knew that downsizing our hectic lifestyle was essential for my health. Although I refused to believe I was dying, I acknowledged the grim truth that my reality was changing.

As we anxiously waited for the ball to drop, the specialist smiled at us and shook his head, "I have good news and bad news. It's not lymphoma.

Actually, I've never seen this before. It's a rare auto-immune disease called Sarcoidosis, and it can mimic lymphoma. I can't help you, but I'll search for someone who can."

"Am I going to die?" I asked.

"I don't think so, but the disease is unpredictable. I can't even give you a prognosis."

Before the internet was popular, information on rare diseases was sketchy. Living in a remote region away from resources also complicated diagnosis and treatment. Our calendar quickly filled with medical appointments as we packed to move into our new home.

In the middle of July, the gallbladder pain interrupted again, necessitating emergency surgery. Our amazing housekeepers jumped in to box our personal belongings at the resort and cleaned and unpacked at the new house. I lay on the couch feeling helpless while I watched the dizzying activity around me.

After moving and settling into our spacious new bungalow in the middle of the quiet forest, we adapted to our new normal. Ron's days off filled with driving me hundreds of miles to a constant stream of appointments. My multidisciplinary medical team monitored me closely as the disease raged, peppering me with prescriptions as symptoms arose. With God's help, I learned to listen to my body and formulated my own treatment plan with rest, diet, and natural medicine.

The illness waxed and waned over the next decade and eventually disappeared from the doctors' radar. Although I never fully recovered my health and I never worked again, I learned to depend on God for the strength and endurance to cope through adversity. Through this process, I've grown to realize that He is always waiting and willing to step into our situation, but we also need to learn to ask for help.

Today, I tell my story to show how God listens to our prayers and sends in support when we need it the most. He cares about the tiniest details of our lives. We need to trust Him, even in the waiting.

I hope my story inspires you to step out in faith and ask God to step into your circumstances.

## QUESTIONS FOR REFLECTION:

> *When you pass through the waters, I will be with you; and through the rivers, they shall not overwhelm you; when you walk through fire you shall not be burned, and the flame shall not consume you."*
> *-Isaiah 43:2*

1. When you reflect on the most difficult time of your life, can you see how God worked in your circumstance for your best interest? Journal your story.

> *When the righteous cry for help, the Lord hears and delivers them out of all their troubles. The Lord is near to the brokenhearted and saves the crushed in spirit."*
> *-Psalm 34:17-18*

2. How do God's promises relieve us from anxiety and fear?

> *Look at the birds of the air; they do not sow or reap or store away in barns, and yet your heavenly Father feeds them. Are you not much more valuable than they?"*
> *-Matthew 6:26.*

3. Jesus said God sees our needs. Can you trust the promises?

∾

As an active tourism operator, social worker and mother of two special needs daughters, Miranda prided herself on her efficiency and problem-solving abilities until a health crisis in 2002 turned her life upside down. After decades of running from Christ, she realized she needed to let go of self-reliance and seek help from a power greater than herself. Her inspiring testimony encourages hope and faith during uncertain times.

Miranda J. Chivers is a Canadian Christian writer and PTSD survivor who seeks to inspire others to overcome difficult circumstances.

**Unequally Yoked**

Staying Committed to Jesus and Your Unbelieving Spouse

Miranda J. Chivers

She is the author of "Unequally Yoked: Staying Committed to Jesus and Your Unbelieving Spouse: Staying Committed to Jesus and Your Unbelieving Spouse" which details the intimate struggles a Christian has when their spouse does not follow Christ. Her ministry includes a support group and mentoring for Christian spouses in unequally yoked marriages. She can be reached through Amazon.com/author/mirandajchivers and social media FB@mirandajchivers.

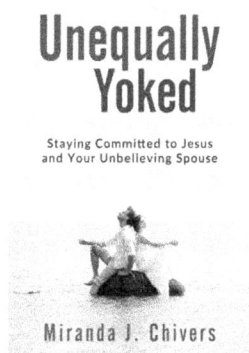

# DRIVEN TOWARD HOPE BY AL AINSWORTH

⚜

> For the creation was subjected to futility, not willingly, but because of him who subjected it, in hope that the creation itself will be set free from its bondage to corruption and obtain the freedom of the glory of the children of God."
> -Romans 8:19-21 (ESV)

The second summer of my marriage brought the first of many summer jobs to fill the gaps of my high school teaching and coaching position. For my wife and me, that summer represented movement toward our goal of becoming debt free. I had paid off her engagement ring, and we had cleared all the balances on our credit cards. All that remained were our two car payments, and the months were clicking away on those. We felt the momentum through the fall, when we discovered my wife was pregnant with our first child. Hope abounded.

I had in mind I would have a son first, we would name him *Michael*, and he would take care of a younger sister or brother in what we planned to one day be a family of four. Our due date was July 4, 1994—conveniently after baseball season and a few weeks before school started back. Perfect.

In retrospect, I should have known my plans would not be what the Lord had in store for us. As with so many other plans I had made for myself and for my family, my plans weren't bad, just different from His. Mine didn't involve the twists and turns His plan would take us through—the rocky places, the opportunities to trust God when the circumstances suggested we shouldn't.

During semester exams for the fall term, I received a phone call at school from my wife. Before the days of cell phones, this was unusual. She was bleeding and needed to go to the doctor to be sure everything was okay. I remember how kind our testing clerk was as I gave her instructions for administering the rest of my exams that day and raced toward the doctor's office. I prayed frantically, not fully understanding what this situation could hold for us and our baby.

My wife and I waited fearfully as the ultrasound technician waved the device over my wife's stomach. We were listening for any positive sign, but she remained silent as she searched for a heartbeat. After what seemed an eternity, she turned to my wife and said, "I'm sorry..." I'm sure more information followed, but those two words told us all we needed. We had lost our child. Hope waned.

This was not a situation we had covered in our pre-marital counseling. A palpable sadness enveloped both of us. I had no idea how to lead my wife through this, and she sat in silence, unable to move one direction or another. When I asked if she needed to get out of the house, she didn't know. When I asked if she wanted to stay home, and she didn't know. I wanted to help so badly it hurt.

But I couldn't make the pain of loss go away. I had no hope to offer, other than the ultimate hope that God would one day cause the mounting sorrow to go away. The Apostle Paul understood the link between suffering and eventual glory. So many of his most encouraging statements to the believer must be taken from the context of his persecution and suffering. His joy and faith and hope weren't rooted in his circumstances, but in his belief beyond what he could see. His hope, his link between this world's suffering and future glory, came through a person, Jesus Christ. Our hope as believers is found in the same source, the same person of Jesus Christ.

We live in a world in which things deteriorate. That brand new car with the new car smell that lingers so long will become a bucket of bolts that can't seem to avoid the shop for more than a month at a time. That new relationship we can't seem to get enough of in the beginning reveals faults and petty annoyances. That new job we once loved so much more than the last one reveals its imperfections, too. Time dashes hope in deteriorating things.

If we're being honest, our hope in Christ is often put to the test again, too. We pray with everything we have for God to save our loved one or release someone from an addiction or heal a relationship, and He doesn't seem to hear. We pray God will change us from the inside out, yet we can't seem to stay out of our own way. A Christian friend or ministry leader betrays us.

Paul understood creation's "bondage to corruption." He examines himself in Romans 7:24 and concludes, "Wretched man that I am! Who will deliver me from this body of death?" Hope is one of the most powerful forces in the world, and Paul seems to have reached the end of his. However, he answers his own anguished cry with his source of hope in the verse that follows his desperate question: "Thanks be to God through Jesus Christ our Lord!"

Paul's hope didn't lie in improving circumstances, just as ours doesn't. His hope lies in a person, but not a spouse or friend or pastor or counselor. His hope comes in Christ alone, the One who overcame sin, death, and the grave. Jesus is the One who promised to come again to make all things right, to usher in a new heaven and a new earth unhindered by sin's curse. How beautiful it will be to one day see the object of our faith and experience our ultimate hope fulfilled.

On the day we lost our baby, I had nothing to offer but my hope in Christ that the curse of sin on this earth wouldn't have the final word. If hope was to rise from our circumstances, it had to come from beyond me. Miscarriages were not discussed in those days. We recalled one other person, one of my wife's best friends from high school, who had miscarried. Her family had just moved that weekend. We couldn't reach out because we didn't have her phone number in those pre-cell phone days, nor her new address. We knew only that her family had moved to one of the largest subdivisions in our county. Attempting to find them would be like trying to find the proverbial needle in a haystack. To add even the stress of not being able to find their house would have been too much. So we stared at the walls.

I cried out to God in my helplessness to show me what to do. So many times, when our first instinct is to do something, the Lord just wants us to come to Him, release our burdens, and abide in Him. This prayer, though, from the emptiness of my soul, led to a one-word instruction in my spirit. Drive. That simple instruction confirmed God heard our prayers, that He hurt with us.

So we drove, not knowing where we would go. We just drove and drove and drove until we turned onto a street leading into Eastover subdivision. Within just a few houses, we saw a familiar van staring at us from their driveway. Of course! If they had just moved, the garage would be full of unpacked belongings. It made perfect sense that there would be no room in the garage for the van. I whispered a prayer of thanks, and we knocked on the door.

Two old friends talked and cried and prayed while their three-year-old daughter read me a stirring version of Little Red Riding Hood in another room. I never asked for specifics of the conversation in the den. All I understood is the Lord provided comfort for my wife through the same comfort with which He had comforted her friend a few years earlier. He lifted my wife from what seemed the beginning of a deep, dark place and gave her hope. Over twenty years later, the Lord reminded me of His kindness when my then twenty-three-year-old reading buddy joined my daughter and I on a mission trip. The memory was one of sadness intermingled with hope that the Lord had shone a light on one of our darkest of days.

I learned through the experience of losing our baby that the Lord is my strength, my hope when all seems lost. The hope wasn't in what He could do for us, though we needed Him to work. Our hope wasn't in my wife's friend, though her experience made her the ideal friend to offer a shoulder of comfort. I learned that when I am helpless, when I have exhausted my last option, He still has resources I can't even imagine. Our ride of faith that day involved just one simple step of obedience on my part. We moved toward our source of hope, and He did the rest.

I wonder, what step of faith do you need to take today to express your hope in Christ? Hebrews 10:23 offers this encouragement:

Let us hold fast the confession of our hope without wavering, for he who promised is faithful." (ESV)

~

Al Ainsworth writes about family, story, and legacy across multiple genres. He is currently working on *Lonesome, Party of Six*, a Christian fiction series that debuted in November 2020.

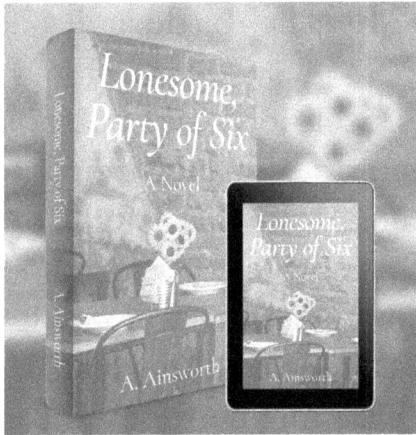

# HOPE, PEACE, AND CANCER-FREE BY EMILY SMITH

❧

"*E*mily Michelle! Little ladies don't talk that loud!"

I've always been loud and outspoken. Some of my earliest memories include being "shushed" and my mother being told that I talked too much in school. Go figure, right? As if she didn't already know! It's funny now though, I can look back over my life and connect the dots. I see God's handiwork in creating me to be who He has called me to be. Little did I know that as an adult my voice would be needed for such a time as this? Facing the unknown I would use my voice to take a stand against an Enemy who was after my life.

"Mrs. Smith, you have a mass in your brain."

I wasn't surprised by this news. I had been

having voracious headaches for a couple of weeks. I wanted everyone to leave and turn off the light. I leaned back on the bed and put a towel over my face thinking it would help with the pain. My husband and I waited patiently for the doctor on call to pay us a visit.

Although the tension was thick in that emergency room that Sunday morning, I had never experienced a more Peace that passes all understanding. It was Mother's Day 2012 I was about to embark on a journey that I never thought would happen to me. God wasn't going to change my situation, but He was going to change my heart.

We should be in church celebrating, but instead we awaited plans for moving forward with a brain tumor.

Have you ever prayed the prayer, "God, use me! I want to be your vessel"?

I laugh when I say be careful what you pray for because He just might do that in the most unexpected ways! I learned that God truly uses *all* things for His good even when we can't see it at first.

The next several hours and days are really a blur. After the initial CT scan that revealed the tumor, we had to make a plan. I have never been a fearful person, but fear tried to grip me as I thought about someone cutting open my head. There's a battle that began in that moment: the battle of Truth vs. Fear. I am a mama, a wife, a daughter, a friend and the thought of missing out on life with my people was real. I realized I had a choice, as we all do, when we face the fear of the unknown.

Would I put my trust in the Savior I professed at the age of 22?

Surgery day came with the emotions you can imagine. Brain surgery is a scary thought! Sitting in the emergency room that first day my mama introduced me to Promise of Psalm 91. It is a Psalm of protection. My favorite verse of this book is Psalm 91:4,

> He will cover you with His feathers, and under His wings you will find refuge; His faithfulness will be your shield and rampart."

Some days were better than others, but I learned to trust in God's faithfulness to cover me. Learning to trust the Lord in His faithfulness is a process. This was step 1 for me. When the thoughts would bombard me, I would pull out my Bible and read this Psalm aloud, sometimes several times at a sitting.

We renew our minds by reading God's Word. It isn't enough to simply "know". We must fill our mind with His promises to face any situation. The most afraid I ever felt during this whole process was when they wheeled me away from my family to enter surgery.

I knew I wasn't alone, that God was with me, but I also knew I was headed into the complete terrain of the unknown. The unknown can be scary! Especially when He's asking you to take a step forward and you can't see the whole path!

Two weeks after surgery I was shopping with my mom. (Crazy, isn't it?!) We were in a Christian bookstore roaming the aisles when Jason called and said I needed to get home. I was a bit aggravated with him as he was cutting our time short! I asked him what was wrong as I could hear the tension in his voice.

He simply replied that I *needed* to get home quickly. Again, true to "Emily style" I told him I couldn't come immediately as I needed to pick up our youngest from his friend's house. Jason reiterated "Emily, come home *now*." I relented and we headed to the house. It's funny, but I think I knew what was coming. I mentally prepared myself as we drove home and prayed, believing God was in complete control and I was healed.

When I walked in Jason was standing in the

kitchen looking pale. Without saying anything I knew what was coming next.

"The nurse called with your results. It's cancer."

I'd like to say that I reacted, but I didn't. I stood there numb. I don't think one is ever fully prepared to hear the words "you've got cancer". I was reminded of the emergency room and the complete Peace that washed over me. I knew this was a pivotal moment in this cancer journey I was embarking on and I chose to believe. I chose to believe God at his Word when He said He would cover me and be my shield and rampart. I chose to believe when God whispered words of healing. I chose to believe my life was not over.

Mother's Day 2012 was one that I will never forget. I accepted Christ as my Savior when I was 22 years old. I thought I knew the Lord. This whole experience thrust me into a new level of relationship with Christ. That's what I was missing: a relationship with Christ.

The next 15 months entailed 17 rounds of chemotherapy and a host of other treatments. Through it all God sustained me. I began reading my Bible and praying daily. Sometimes I would sit with the Bible on top of me because I didn't know what to read or what to pray. That's the beauty of Jesus. He knows what we need even when we don't. Learning to relay and trust on Him is a process.

For some of us we must hit bottom to learn that trust. He is ever patient waiting on us. He knew our days before we even born! He knew what we would face, yet he allows us to choose. I chose to stand on The Word of God and trust His timing.

If I learned anything it was this: God is good even in the bad. God is not a God of sickness and disease. I want to be clear about this, God uses ALL things for His glory if we will allow Him. So, I pose the question to you. Will you be willing to let God use *anything* for His glory to show the world He is faithful? All He needs is willing vessels.

My first oncologist told me he would "never" pronounce me cancer free. I remember being stunned at his statement, but I also remember a still small voice telling me otherwise. I was pronounced cancer free in September 2013, not by my first oncologist but another. God is faithful to His children. He has a purpose and plan for me and for you. Since my cancer I am living a full and rich life of Peace. Peace is a Person named Jesus Christ. We just need to trust and believe that He will make a way. He did for me and I know He will for you. Keep fighting, warrior.

~

Emily lives in Mississippi with her husband, Jason, and two sons Cade and Noah. She hosts the blog Song of a Sparrow. Emily is a writer, blogger, speaker, and Bible study leader. Answering the call to "Who will go?" led her to help people Jesus can use all things for His glory.

Blog: www.songofasparrow.org, also on Facebook as Song of a Sparrow Blog by Emily Smith

Instagram: @song_of_a_sparrow

# WHEN HOPE SEEMS LOST
## BY PAM PEGRAM

here wasn't a tragic accident, nothing terrible happened, actually there was much to be thankful for, but I found myself downcast and struggling. Something I had longed for as long as I could remember was so close, yet the realization was hitting that it would never be mine. Matter of fact, it was further away than I ever imagined it could be. It hurt.

At first, I felt devastation. It was so hard to understand and make it make sense – at least from my perspective. But as time passed, in spite of wise counsel and praying friends, I found myself stuck. I was stuck in my pain, stuck in my resentment, and even stuck feeling I had been wronged. It didn't happen overnight, but before I knew it, I grew bitter.

The exact details and cause of what I experienced really don't matter. Maybe you can relate. There hasn't been a life-shattering event, or a loss of a loved one, or a season of great suffering. Maybe what is bothering you is not huge, it's small in comparison to what others have experienced. Yet, you feel downcast and as if all hope is lost.

What has brought you here? Are you struggling with unmet expectations… harsh criticism from those you just want to love you… your need to be included or acknowledged… your hard work not paying off for you and your family… the approval you desperately crave, but will never receive… the desires of your heart not being granted… poor decisions you are forced to live with… a diagnosis you never wanted…the fairytale that only exists in your dreams?

There is much in this world that can tempt us to lose sight of our hope and instead enter into a place of despair.

There are times when it just feels like too much. We talk about it more than we should. Our mind plays and replays scenarios over and over again and just when we take our eyes off of it and try to lay it down, Satan hisses and brings it all rushing right back to our memory. We might even over dramatize it... just a little.

When we find ourselves discouraged, bitter, or downcast it is a good indicator that we have lost our primary focus. Maybe we recognize this is happening or maybe we don't. Maybe we know we need to let it go. But maybe, just maybe – that feels like too much to ask us to do. Or sometimes we are ready to release it, but before it rolls off the tip of our fingers, we snatch it right back up and cling to it with all of our might. Are you identifying with this or just thinking that this girl needs a lot of counseling?

My guess is – you get it. If you aren't there right now, you have been or you will be sometime in the near future. So, what are we to do? What is it that God expects of us? One of my favorite passages in the Bible is Romans 5:2-5 where Paul writes:

> Therefore, having been justified by faith, we have peace with God through our Lord Jesus Christ, through whom also we have access by faith into this grace in which we stand, and rejoice in hope of the glory of God. And not only that, but we also glory in tribulations, knowing that tribulation produces

perseverance; and perseverance, character; and character, hope. Now hope does not disappoint, because the love of God has been poured out in our hearts by the Holy Spirit who was given to us."

Immediately, this scripture brings us back to our starting point; back to the moment of our salvation when we were reconciled with God. Shouldn't that moment – that one defining moment impact every other moment from that point forward? It was then, that we made peace with God and our life shifted from being all about me to being all about Him. Yet, we teeter totter and go back and forth – all about Him, all about me, all about Him, all about me.

We will get back to the passage in Romans in a moment. But here is a question for you – why is it that we expect our faith journey to be a smooth one? Why are we so surprised when we find ourselves struggling to maintain intimacy with our Savior, struggling to have hope? Jesus warned us that Satan is here to steal, kill and destroy us any way he can. One of those ways is to distract us from the hope that we have in Christ.

I was distracted alright. Satan was making sure of it. He had a plan and he had waged a war. I was in the Word, I was praying fervently about my situation, and I was seeking counsel from only those few who would offer Biblically sound advice. Yet, still I struggled. You see, Satan doesn't have to make us become bad – he just needs to keep us focused on everything else instead of God. And the truth is – even though I was going through the motions of doing what is right – my thoughts were swirling – I was listening to his hisses. They were swirling around and around and around – pulling me down and down and deeper still into a pit I had no business entering.

This is nothing new. We can remember these types of struggles all throughout our lives, can't we? Childhood wounds, marital woes, adulting struggles, family scars, friends who have unfriended us, and on and on. Even the psalmist was no stranger to discouragement when he wrote about the place he was in and reminded himself of the answer,

> Why are you downcast, O my soul?
> And why are you disquieted within me?
> Hope in God, for I shall yet praise
> Him for the help of His countenance.
> O my God, my soul is cast down within
> me; therefore, I will remember You."
> -Psalm 42:5-6

Here is what I know—the answer is always Jesus, the Truth never changes, and we can always stand on the promises of God.

My struggle continued far too long. I allowed it to become much harder than it ever should have been. I gave my feelings power and let them mislead me. Hmmm... why am I admitting this in a book for all to see? Here I am – a believer who blogs about focusing on what matters most – our relationship with Jesus – and I let my feelings, my circumstances, my pain matter more. I am sharing because we are all the same – flawed, broken and in need of Jesus.

And nothing matters more than sharing Him, talking about who He is and what He has done, with others. That is pretty much why we are here. What if your pain is what leads you to share Him with someone who otherwise might not ever come to know Him?

Now, back to our passage in Romans... my study Bible has the title, *Faith Triumphs in Trouble* just above the start of Chapter 5. See God knows that this life is a battle and He has given us all that we need to endure, to get through, and even to triumph during difficult times. He has promised to use every hard day for our good if and when we get out of the way and surrender our struggle to Him.

Believers can rejoice in the hope they have. You

see this hope is not just wishful thinking. When we *hope in the Lord* we have a confident expectation that He is who He says He is and that He will do all that He has promised. When we take our eyes off our tribulations and instead focus on Him, we remember the glory of God and all our struggles quickly pale in comparison to Him.

It is the tribulations – the struggles, the hard seasons, the disappointments – that God uses to produce perseverance in us. It is what send us running to Him. It is what grows our faith in Him and gives us the strength to endure whatever this world throws at us. If all we experienced were good days, faith would not be required. If we never experience anything bad, how could we possibly understand the goodness of God and the hope we have in Him?

As we continue, our perseverance produces character – which is the quality of being approved. Read that again – the *quality of being approved*. If God has approved us – then why are we so desperately seeking the approval of others. Stop it. We don't need it. We have been given all we need. We just need to embrace it. Our worth, our value and our identity have nothing to do with who we are and what we have done; but instead it is found in who Jesus is and what He has done for us.

When we walk with God through the hard

times, He works in us and develops qualities and virtues that strengthen us and draw us closer to Him. There is nothing better than that. We grow to know God more – to understand His character and the love He has for us. He is using this season to build our character and fortify our hope in Him and in all of His promises to us.

The reason that we can be so confident is that the love of God has been poured out. The moment we trusted in Christ we received the Holy Spirit who constantly encourages us in our hope in God. We have hope. It is never lost, only misplaced. We just need to pause and remember where it is. If we are downcast, we are looking in all the wrong places and just need to look up. Look up and be reminded where you can find hope.

So, how does my story end? It is ongoing until I am standing face to face with my Creator. But things changed as God convicted me that my feelings were causing me to sin and plant a root of bitterness. So – I repented of my ways and began allowing those I trust to speak truth to me – even when I didn't want to hear it. I sought wise counsel to help me find a way to endure and to honor God with my attitude and even my thoughts. I stopped focusing on how BIG my hurts were and instead focused on how much BIGGER my God is. I still teeter totter every now and then, but it is short lived. This life I am living is filled with blessings. Yes, there are challenges, hard days and even tears, disappointments and pain, and a few fears. But nothing I will experience compares to the hope I have – the joy that is mine – because I know how my story ends. Do you? If not – you can. Let's continue reading in Romans 5. Verse 6-11 tells us:

> For when we were still without strength, in due time Christ died for the ungodly. For scarcely for a righteous man will one die; yet perhaps for a good man someone would even dare to die. But God demonstrates His own love toward us in that while we were still sinners, Christ died for us. Much more then, having now been justified by His blood, we shall be saved from wrath through Him. For if when we were enemies we were reconciled to God through the death of His Son, much more, having been reconciled, we shall be saved by His life. And not only that, but we also rejoice in God through our Lord Jesus Christ, through whom we have not received the reconciliation."

Friends, Hope has a name, His name is Jesus!

# THE GARDEN OF HOPE BY MICHAEL LACEY

*Do* you need a prescription for hope? Not as in, "I'm suffering from hope, please help me." Nobody would say something like that. Well, maybe some of us hopeless romantics, but that's another story.

I won't leave you hanging. There is one thing you must do to increase your hope: worship.

***Praise is the prescription for hope.*** The garden of hope requires praise foremost, then as consequence of praise: grace, wisdom, faith, and proper perspectives.

Firstly, let us acknowledge this truth:

> As Christ's kingdom is not of this world, so is not our hope. The worldling's motto is, "a bird in the hand." Give me today, say they, and take tomorrow whoso will. But the word of believers is, spero meliora—my hopes are better than my present possessions."
> -Elnathan Parr

I'll warn you up front. This particular devotional story will be filled with incredible quotes and writings from great men of God. I'm simply delivering the words the Holy Spirit has inspired me to hold onto lately. To find hope, learn how to praise. To learn how to praise, go to the Psalms and their incredible depth and insight.

Charles Spurgeon—a great scholar but also the source of my current studies—says of Psalm 27, ***"It is a song of cheerful hope, well fitted for those in trial who have learned to lean upon the Almighty arm."***

How is praise supposed to build hope? Well, it builds more than just hope. Hope becomes a byproduct, or perhaps even a fruit, of well-placed praise.

We know this: God desires to be known, to be worshiped. Through reading His word, praying to

Him, praising, and worshiping, we know more of Him and His attributes, His qualities. In knowing Him more, we trust Him more. In all of those things, we see His faithfulness. And in knowing He is faithful, we grow in faith. At some point, we can't help but hope, because we begin to know what waits on the other side of each trial, each storm, each hardship.

God waits on the other side with open arms. He stands next to us hand-in-hand, and He goes before us with His mighty right hand.

Storms are not timid, they are not tame, and they do not care who they affect. However, our God is not timid, He is certainly not tame, but He does care. William S. Plumer wrote, ***"Hope in God. The more terrible the storm, the more necessary is the anchor."***

> We have this hope as an anchor for the soul, firm and secure."
> Hebrews 6:19a (CSV)

These men knew something about hope that often alludes so many of us. Let's go deeper.

> Why am I agitated like a troubled sea, and why do my thoughts make a noise like a tumultuous multitude? The causes are not enough to justify such utter yielding to despondency. Up, my heart! What aileth thee? Play the man, and thy castings down shall turn to up liftings, and thy disquietudes to calm. ***Hope*** thou in God. If every evil be let loose from Pandora's box, yet is there ***hope*** at the bottom." -Spurgeon

In Psalms 42:5 and 43:5, the word "disquieted" is more literally "tumultuated," as in the tossing of the roaring, tumultuous sea.

> Why are you cast down, O my soul? And why are you disquieted within me? Hope in God, for I shall yet praise Him for the help of His countenance."
> -Psalm 42:5; 43:5 (NKJV)

When we read this verse, we don't think of our sorrows. We grow in hope. Our hope lays sorrow's assertions and arguments to rest. Faith disproves fears rebuttals.

Even though I walk through the valley
of the shadow of death, I fear no evil,
for You are with me; Your rod and Your
staff, they comfort me."
    -Psalm 23:4 (NASB)

When we read this chapter, we don't think
about the valley of the shadow of death, we think
about the Good Shepherd who is with us, always
has been, and always will be, as He leads us along
the right paths.

You intended to harm me, but God
intended it for good to accomplish
what is now being done, the saving of
many lives."
    -Genesis 50:20 (NIV)

When we read this passage, we're reminded
that God works even the most dire circumstances
for our good.

It is the darkness, the difficulty, the despair the
drive us a God who pours hope out like He does
His grace. And it is his grace that becomes the
foundation for unshakable hope. Through praise,
we recognize His grace. Through grace, we see
through the world's economy to something much
greater. By grace, we walk with hope.

Once again, Spurgeon's words honor God and shed light:

"This is the grace that swims, though the waves roar and be troubled. God is unchangeable, and therefore his grace is the ground for unshaken hope. If everything be dark, yet the day will come, and meanwhile **hope carries stars in her eyes;** her lamps are not dependent on oil from without, her light is fed by secret visitations of God, which sustain the spirit.

**For I shall yet praise him**. Yet will my sighs give place to songs, my mournful ditties shall be exchanged for triumphal paeans. A loss of the present sense of God's love is not a loss of that love itself; the jewel is there, though it gleams not on our breast; **hope** knows her title good when she cannot read it clear; she expects the promised boon though present providence stands before her with empty hands.

**For I shall yet praise him** for the help of his countenance. Salvations come from the propitious face of God, and he will yet lift up his countenance upon us.

Note well that the main **hope** and chief desire of David rest in the smile of God. His face is what he seeks and **hopes** to see, and this will recover his low spirits, this will put to scorn his laughing enemies, this will restore to him all the joys of those holy and happy days around which memory lingers. This is grand cheer. This verse, like the singing of Paul and Silas, looses chains and shakes prison walls. He who can use such heroic language in his gloomy hours will surely conquer. In the garden of **hope** grow the laurels for future victories, the roses of coming joy, the lilies of approaching peace...

Wherefore indulge unreasonable sorrows, which benefit no one, fret thyself, and dishonour thy God? Why overburden thyself with forebodings? **Hope** in God, or wait for God. There is need of patience, but there is ground for **hope**. The Lord cannot but avenge his own elect. The heavenly Father will not stand by and see his children trampled on for ever; as surely as the sun is in the heavens, light must arise for the people of God, though for awhile they may walk in darkness. Why, then, should we not be encouraged, and lift up our head with comfortable hope?

***For I shall yet praise him***. Times of complaint will soon end, and seasons of praise will begin. Come, my heart, look out of the window, borrow the telescopic glass, forecast a little, and sweeten thy chamber with sprigs of the sweet herb of ***hope***. Who is the health of my countenance, and my God. My God will clear the furrows from my brow, and the tear marks from my cheek; therefore will I lift up my head and smile in the face of the storm."

One of the tenets of worship—and the Christian life— is to get outside of ourselves. When we fix our eyes on Jesus, the things of this world fade away. When we strive to be like Him, we begin to seek out ways to serve rather than to be served. Erwin McManus, in his devotional from The Way of the Warrior, writes beautifully about this shift as he equates selflessness to wisdom and wisdom to hope.

"The warrior wields a weapon only to
defend, protect, and liberate. When the
warrior is wise, they fight only for peace.
Where there is wisdom, there is always
hope. Wisdom simplifies. Wisdom
clarifies. Wisdom untangles. Wisdom
unshackles. Wisdom illuminates...This
is the highest expression of wisdom—to
live our lives for others rather than
ourselves...
It is a small thing to simply fight for
yourself when there are so many who
need your battle cry...
What is done for ourselves will one day be
forgotten, but that what we have done
for others will be remembered for
eternity."

Let us look not in or even around, not at first.
Let us look up, to God who is in the heavens and
does as He pleases (Psalm 115:3). Let us praise the
Maker, the Creator, the Majestic. As we focus on
Him, our priorities step in line. As we look to the
King, our reverence deepens. As we acknowledge
the goodness and power of God, our faith grows.
As we grow to know Him more, we walk in
wisdom, in grace, and by His nature, in hope.

Tend the garden with praise, and don't be

overwhelmed when you begin to hope for things immeasurable and beyond the scope of your imagination.

~

Michael Lacey is (mostly) responsible for producing these Christian Writers' Collections.

Most of this is done without compensation, so any help is appreciated. If you're an author, reach out to him through his author services business, Story Builds Creative, where he helps creatives build their stories and get their works and words into the world.

Fill out Michael's author survey at StoryBuildsCreative.com to book a free clarity session for your own writing project. You can also email him at michael@michaellacey.me for any questions concerning faith, writing, and creative pursuits OR to follow along with the next Christian Writers' collection and contribute time and/or finances!

Sign up at ChristWriters.com.

# FREE DEVOTIONALS AND STORIES

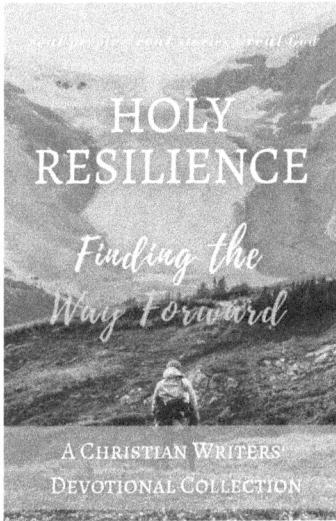

Want the next Christian Writers' Collection—Holy Resilience: Finding the Way Forward—for free!?

Join the advance reader team at

**read.ChristWriters.com**

to get special access to each new collection, including authors from this one and more. You'll only be subscribed to this one list. If you wish to receive updates from specific authors, follow the links at the end of their devotional stories.

By subscribing, you'll get:

- advance copies of upcoming Christian Writers' Collections
- special digital gift offers from the authors
- opportunities to vote on devo topics and charities
- chances to win competitions and more!

# JOIN THE NEXT COLLECTION

Are you an author or writer? You don't have to be published or self-published; you just need a heart after God and a word to share.

More info at ChristWriters.com. Also, join our Facebook Group, Christian Writers' Collections: (facebook.com/groups/christiancollections). to follow along and see how you can contribute!

Special thanks to Story-Builds.com (Story Builds Creative) for organizing and producing this book in conjunction with Christian Writer's Collections. Contact michael@michaellacey.me if you have ANY self-publishing needs!

## LAST REQUEST

If any of the words in these devotionals has helped you, please leave an honest review on Amazon. This will help get these life-changing stories and teachings into more hands!